SQE 1 PREP COURSE

TORT

BY ANASTASIA & ANDREW VIALICHKA

First Edition

Published by MetExam
https://metexam.co.uk

(m)etexam

ISBN: 978-1-917053-05-1

ISBN: 978-1-917053-27-3 (Hardcover Book)

The information provided in this book is subject to change without notice and should not be construed as a commitment by the authors or the publisher. While every effort has been made to ensure the accuracy of the information contained herein, the authors and publisher assume no responsibility for any errors or omissions, or for damages resulting from the use of the information contained in this book.

This publication is designed exclusively for educational purposes, serving as a comprehensive study aid for individuals preparing for the SQE 1 examination. It should not be construed as offering legal advice or as an authoritative resource on legal matters. Its primary objective is to facilitate learning and exam preparation.

Authors: Vialichka, Anastasia; Vialichka, Andrew
Title: Tort. SQE 1 Prep Course / Anastasia Vialichka, Andrew Vialichka
Description: First Edition | London: MetExam, 2024
Identifiers: ISBN 978-1-917053-05-1
Subjects: LCSH Tort Law—United Kingdom—Examinations, questions, etc. | Tort Law—England—Examinations, questions, etc. | Tort Law—Wales—Examinations, questions, etc. | Negligence—United Kingdom—Examinations, questions, etc. | Personal Injury Law—England—Examinations, questions, etc. | Legal Liability—Wales—Examinations, questions, etc. | Legal education—United Kingdom.

INTRODUCTION

Welcome to the foundational stone of your journey to-wards becoming a solicitor in England and Wales. This text is meticulously crafted as part of a comprehensive MetExam training course designed to prepare you for the Solicitors Qualifying Examination. It lays out the intricate legal tapestry you are about to navigate, providing you with the essential knowledge and analytical tools needed to succeed.

Embrace the learning that awaits, and let this book be your guide and ally on the path to legal proficiency and excellence.

Throughout this text, authors draw upon a wealth of legal scholarship and case law. While specific contributions are not cited in the body of the book, a comprehensive list of all works referenced can be found at the end. These references serves as an acknowledgment of the significant works that have informed this text and as a resource for readers seeking to explore the subject matter further.

CHAPTER 1.
DELIBERATE INTRU-
SION INTO LAND (IN-
TENTIONAL TORTS)

1. Intrusion onto Property - Trespass to Land

An act of trespass to land is characterised by an unauthorised and direct intrusion upon the land that a claimant lawfully possesses. Notably, to establish a case of trespass to land, the claimant doesn't need to demonstrate actual harm or damage to the property. The mere encroachment of the claimant's proprietary rights suffices for legal action.

1.1 Fundamental Components

(a) **Possession.** To initiate a legal claim of trespass to land, the claimant must hold exclusive possession of the land.

Sarah, who holds a lease to an apartment, finds that her neighbour, Tom, has been using her rooftop patio without permission. Sarah's exclusive lease grants her possession rights despite not owning the property, making Tom's actions a potential trespass case.

(b) **Land.** The protection against trespass extends to the land and any structures erected upon it. This protection is not limited to the land's surface but also encompasses the subsurface and the airspace above the land to a height reasonably necessary for the ordinary utilisation of the land and its structures.

Instances of trespass may include actions like:

- Undertaking subterranean excavation from an individual's land that extends beneath a neighbouring property.

- Manoeuvring a crane or piloting a drone into the airspace of a neighbour's property.

A local construction company inadvertently extends its excavation activities beneath John's property while working on an adjacent site. This act constitutes a trespass, infringing on John's subsurface rights.

(c) **Direct Interference.** For an action to be categorised as trespass, there must be a direct physical intrusion or interference. Such natural intrusions include unlawfully entering the land, crossing it by vehicle, forcibly seizing it, placing objects, or depositing materials onto it. Permitting one's animals to enter someone else's property also constitutes direct trespass.

In contrast, **indirect interference** is not deemed to be trespass. This includes situations where a tree planted on one's land extends its roots or branches into a neighbouring land or disturbances caused by noise, vibrations, or odours. Rather than constituting trespass, these scenarios may lead to a legal claim under the category of nuisance, which is discussed in a later section.

A farmer, Mr. Brown, discovers that his neighbour's cattle have broken through a fence and are grazing on his land. This direct physical intrusion by the animals is a clear case of trespass.

(d) **Intention.** An act of trespass to land usually involves a deliberate act of encroachment. The crux of the matter is the intention to enter the land, irrespective of whether the individual intended to commit trespass or was aware of the land's rightful ownership. Thus, a defence based on a mistaken belief regarding land ownership or authorisation to enter the land is generally ineffective.

If a hiker, believing a trail to be public land, accidentally wanders onto private property, they have committed trespass. The hiker's lack of intent to trespass is irrelevant; the critical factor is their intentional act of entering the land.

1.2 Defences to Trespass to Land

(a) **Authorised Entry.** One of the primary defences against a trespass to land accusation is when the entry is authorised under law, in instances where

legal provisions or statutory rights back the defendant's presence on the property, the act does not constitute trespass.

> A scenario where a utility worker enters a property under the
> powers conferred by utility legislation, even without the direct
> consent of the property owner, would not be considered
> trespass, as the entry is legally sanctioned.

(b) **Emergency Necessity.** The defence of emergency necessity is applicable in cases where the defendant's intrusion onto the claimant's property is
crucial to prevent immediate danger to life or significant property damage. This could include situations where a person enters the property without
permission to control or prevent a disaster, such as
halting a rapidly spreading fire, or to avoid imminent danger, like dodging an out-of-control vehicle.

In these circumstances, the pressing need to avert
serious harm or threat justifies the otherwise unauthorised entry onto the land, thus providing a legal
defence against the charge of trespass.

1.3 Legal Remedies for Trespass to Land

(a) **Award of Damages.** Given that trespass to land
is inherently actionable (actionable per se), the
claimant is invariably eligible for a minimum of
nominal damages in every trespass instance. This is
particularly pertinent when the claimant's objective

is to validate their legal ownership of the land, which they allege the defendant has infringed upon. In scenarios where the trespass results in measurable loss or damage, the court may award compensatory damages to mirror the actual loss suffered by the claimant.

(b) **Issuance of an Injunction.** The court can issue an injunction against the defendant to prevent ongoing or future trespassing. This legal directive acts as a deterrent, barring the defendant from further unauthorised entry or activities on the claimant's property.

(c) **Legal Action for Recovery of Land – Possession Order.** Suppose the claimant, rightfully entitled to land, has been ousted by the defendant. In that case, they can initiate legal action to affirm their title and seek a court-mandated order for regaining possession of the land.

This process involves establishing their legal right to the land and obtaining judicial assistance to reclaim their possession.

(d) **Limited Scope of Self-Help.** While the principle of self-help theoretically allows a rightful possessor of land to use reasonable force to remove a trespasser, this method is tightly regulated. The law prohibits the use of violence or the threat of violence to re-enter premises that are occupied by another, except in the case of a displaced residential occupier.

Consequently, the practical application of self-help as a remedy is significantly limited. Pursuing a court order for possession is typically more prudent, considering the legal restrictions and potential risks associated with self-help measures.

2. Infringements to the Person

Trespass to the person is a legal category that includes three separate but related torts: battery, assault, and false imprisonment. Each of these torts is inherently actionable without demonstrating specific harm or damage. Their fundamental purpose is to protect against unauthorised intrusions on an individual's physical autonomy and integrity.

Consequently, any infringement upon the claimant's right to personal security and bodily integrity suffices to establish a basis for legal action.

2.1 Battery as an Infringement of Personal Security

Battery is identified as the intentional and direct application of illegitimate force to another's body.

(a) **Illegitimate Force.** This encompasses any physical contact made without the other person's consent. Activities ranging from non-consensual touching to providing medical treatment against someone's will fall under this category.

If an individual forcibly hugs another person who has clearly expressed their objection to such contact, it constitutes battery due to the absence of consent.

(b) **Direct Physical Contact.** The essence of a battery lies in the directness of the contact. This includes physically striking someone, grabbing them, or throwing an object that contacts their body or clothing.

Directly pushing someone, resulting in physical contact, is a precise instance of battery.

(c) **Deliberate Action.** The action leading to contact must be intentional; accidental or involuntary actions do not qualify as battery.

Accidentally bumping into someone in a crowded space does not amount to battery, as the contact was not intentional.

(d) **Intent to Apply Force, Not to Harm.** In battery cases, it's the intent to apply key force, not necessarily to cause harm. The individual is liable for all direct consequences of their action, regardless of their intention to harm.

A prankster throws a water balloon at someone, intending to get them wet, but the impact causes an injury. This is a battery, as the intention was to apply force, even though the harm was not intended.

(e) **Doctrine of Transferred Intent.** This principle applies when the intention to use force on one person inadvertently results in a force being applied to another.

If a person throws a stone aiming to hit a specific target but unintentionally hits a different person, the original intent to apply force is transferred to the unintended victim, constituting battery.

2.2 Assault in Violation of Personal Security

An assault occurs when there is an intentional act that leads the claimant to reasonably anticipate the immediate and direct application of unlawful force upon themselves (essentially, the fear of an impending battery).

(a) **Intentional Act.** The defendant must have intended to create the expectation of impending force in the claimant.

(b) **Apprehension of Force.** The claimant must be conscious of the threat of force; if they are unaware, no assault has occurred. For instance, if the defendant strikes the claimant from behind without prior warning, this would be considered battery but not assault.

- **Differentiating from Fear.** 'Apprehension' of force implies an expectation of force, not necessarily a state of fear.

- **Force Not Required to be Actualised.** An assault can occur even without the physical application of force. For example, if the defendant raises their arm to strike the claimant but is stopped before making contact, this still constitutes an assault despite the absence of actual battery.

- **Reasonableness of Apprehension.** The claimant's anticipation of imminent force must be reasonable. If it's clear that the defendant cannot execute the threat, then it does not amount to assault.

- **Role of Verbal Threats.** Verbal threats can constitute an assault if they present an immediate threat of force. For instance, threatening phone calls can be seen as assault if the claimant reasonably believes the threat could be executed imminently. Conversely, words can also negate an assault; for example, if the defendant brandishes a clenched fist but accompanies it with words indicating no immediate intent to strike, the threat of direct force is nullified, and thus, there is no assault.

2.3 False Imprisonment as an Infringement of Personal Security

False imprisonment occurs when there is an illegal restriction on the claimant's ability to move freely from a specific location.

(a) **Illegality of Constraint.** The term 'false' in false imprisonment signifies that the restriction on the claimant must be unlawful. The presence of lawful justification for the detainment of the claimant serves as a defence against a claim of false imprisonment.

For instance, if the defendant has legal authority or a legitimate reason, such as a police officer arresting under valid circumstances, the detainment may not be considered false imprisonment.

(b) **Intentionality of Constraint.** For a false imprisonment case to stand, the defendant's actions that restricted the claimant's movement must be deliberate. The defendant doesn't need to have intended the constraint to be illegal. A mistaken belief by the defendant that they had the legal authority to detain the claimant does not serve as a valid defence. In essence, what matters is the intention to confine, not the perception of the legality of such confinement.

(c) **Total Restriction on Movement.** In the context of false imprisonment, the essence lies in the complete limitation of the claimant's ability to move freely. To constitute false imprisonment, the constraint on movement must be total, preventing the claimant from moving in any direction. Should the claimant be able to move freely in any direction or have access to a feasible means of escape, it negates the criteria for false imprisonment. The critical aspect is the absence of any practical option for the claimant to move or exit from the place of confinement freely.

(d) **Knowledge of Constraint Not Required.** For a claim of false imprisonment, the claimant doesn't have to be aware of the constraint at the time it occurs. The primary focus of this tort is to safeguard the claimant's right to freedom of movement, irrespective of their awareness of the restriction.

Therefore, the legality of the claim hinges on the actual restriction of movement, not on the claimant's perception or awareness of such restriction.

2.4 Legal Defences in Cases of Trespass to the Person

(a) **Consent as a Defence.** The defence of consent is crucial in trespass to the person cases. The claimant's agreement to the physical contact effectively negates allegations of trespass.

- **Consent in the Context of Medical Treatment.** A mentally capable adult has the autonomous right to refuse medical intervention, even if such refusal could be life-threatening. Therefore, consent is necessary for medical procedures to avoid characterising the act as a battery.

- **Implied Consent in Certain Situations.** In activities like sports, participants are generally assumed to have implicitly agreed to the level of physical contact that is inherent and expected in the ordinary course of the game, provided it adheres to the game's rules. This implied consent does not extend to contacts that violate the rules. Furthermore, if an injury results from negligent conduct during play, a claim under the tort of negligence may be applicable.

- **Constraints on Consent.** Consent must be free from coercion, deceit, or significant misinformation to be valid. Additionally, public policy considerations may invalidate consent to extreme forms of physical harm, indicating that legal consent for such harm may not be recognised, even if the claimant accepts it willingly.

(b) **Necessity as a Defence.** The defence of necessity is applicable when the defendant's actions, undertaken to prevent harm, are reasonable under the circumstances. For instance, in cases where an adult cannot give consent for medical treatment due to a lack of capacity, specific statutes outline the conditions under which such treatment can be lawfully administered. In these situations, these statutory provisions offer a legal defence against claims of battery that might otherwise arise from non-consensual medical intervention.

(c) **Self-Defence as a Legal Defence in Trespass Cases.** Self-defence is a valid defence in trespass to the person cases, applicable when the defendant can substantiate that their actions were in response to an actual or reasonably perceived imminent attack by the claimant.

- **Proportionality of Force.** The force employed in self-defence must be proportionate and reasonable relative to the threat or aggression encountered. Excessive force beyond what is necessary to repel the attack may not qualify under this defence.

- **Extension to Protecting Others and Property.** Self-defence also encompasses actions taken to protect other individuals or to defend one's property. However, the scope of reasonable force is typically more constrained in property defence scenarios than in personal or third-party defence. This implies a higher threshold for justifying the level of force used when the defence is centred around property rather than personal safety.

(d) **Lawful Arrest and Lawful Authority as Defences.** In cases of trespass to the person, the act of conducting a lawful arrest or acting under legal authority provides a defence. This means that actions which might otherwise be considered battery or false imprisonment can be legally justified under certain circumstances.

- **Lawful Arrest.** Actions such as physically detaining a person, which could typically constitute battery and false imprisonment, are defensible if they occur during a lawful arrest. In this context, the legality of the arrest is crucial in determining the legitimacy of the physical actions taken.

- **Imprisonment Under Statutory Power.** A defence to false imprisonment is also present when a person is detained under a specific statutory authority. This includes situations where individuals are legally incarcerated following a court sentence or are held in custody pending trial. In these cases, the statutory basis for the detention serves as a legal justification, rendering the con-

finement lawful and not a case of false imprisonment.

2.5 Remedies for Trespass to the Person – Damages

Trespass to the person is inherently actionable, allowing for legal action even without proving actual harm.

Consequently, even if the claimant hasn't sustained any tangible damage, they are still eligible to receive an award of nominal damages.

(a) **Compensatory Damages for Actual Harm.**
In instances where the claimant has endured actual damage, such as physical injury, they can be awarded compensatory damages. These damages are intended to correlate with and compensate for the harm suffered directly.

(b) **Damages for Non-Physical Harm.** Additionally, damages can be awarded for non-physical implications of the trespass, like the humiliation or inconvenience experienced by the claimant. This acknowledges that the impact of trespass on the person can extend beyond physical injuries, warranting compensation for these broader effects.

3. Direct Interference with Personal Property

Trespass to goods occurs when there is a purposeful and direct intervention in the claimant's control or ownership of personal property. This form of trespass addresses the unauthorised and intentional disruption of a claimant's rights over their tangible assets.

(a) **Forms of Interference.** Trespass to goods encompasses a range of actions, from physically taking the goods to causing damage or simply meddling with them in some way, such as moving them without permission. Even minor actions like touching the goods can constitute trespass if they exceed the bounds of typical, everyday handling. Examples include deliberate acts like scratching a vehicle or unauthorised application of a wheel clamp to impede its movement.

(b) **Requirement of Intention.** For an action to be considered trespass to goods, the defendant must have willfully engaged in the act that interferes with the goods. The critical factor is the intention to carry out the act rather than an intention to commit trespass per se. Therefore, a mistaken belief regarding ownership of the goods does not serve as a defence against a trespass claim.

(c)   **Absence of Damage Requirement.** While actual damage to the goods is not a prerequisite for a trespass claim, the presence of such damage can lead to an award of damages reflecting the extent of the loss incurred. This provision accommodates claims where the trespass results in quantifiable damage, allowing for appropriate compensation.

Legal Recourse for Trespass to Goods:

In cases of trespass to goods, action can be taken regardless of whether actual loss has been incurred. Where no tangible loss is evident, the claimant may still be eligible for nominal damages, symbolising the recognition of the infringement of their rights over the goods.

When the trespass leads to discernible damage, such as physical harm to the goods or disruption in their utilisation, compensatory damages can be pursued. These damages are intended to financially reflect the extent and impact of the damage caused by the trespass.

In situations where the claimant has been deprived of the goods due to the trespass, the compensation awarded should be based on the current market value of the goods. This approach ensures that the claimant receives a monetary sum that accurately represents the value of the lost goods.

4. Explanation of Conversion

The tort of conversion occurs when an individual handles goods in a manner that significantly contradicts the owner's rights.

(a) **Intentional Act.** It must be shown that the defendant intentionally carried out the act that interfered with the goods. The critical aspect here is the intention behind the action, not an intent to violate ownership rights. Consequently, even if the defendant mistakenly believed they owned the goods or had the right to use them, this does not excuse the act of conversion.

If John borrows Alice's laptop without her permission and sells it, believing it was his laptop due to its similar appearance, this constitutes conversion. John's selling the laptop significantly breaches Alice's ownership rights and his mistaken belief about the laptop's ownership doesn't negate the conversion.

(b) **Acts Constituting Conversion.** Conversion occurs when a defendant's actions deeply infringe upon the owner's rights, effectively denying the owner the use and possession of their goods. Such acts include illegal acquisition (like theft), unauthorised transfer, wrongful retention, significant alteration, severe damage, or misuse of personal property (chattel).

It's important to note that conversion doesn't cover trivial disturbances, such as minor scratches on someone else's car. For these lesser interferences, the relevant legal action is trespass to goods, not conversion.

(c) **Distinction and Overlap with Trespass to Goods.** While trespass to goods involves direct interference with the possession of the goods, conversion is characterised by actions that fundamentally contradict the owner's rights. There can be instances where trespass to goods and conversion co-occur, depending on the nature and extent of the interference with the goods.

Remedies for Conversion:

When addressing conversion, the remedies available depend on whether the defendant still possesses the claimant's goods:

(a) **Defendant Retains Possession of Goods.** The court may order the defendant to return the goods to the claimant. Compensation equivalent to the fair market value of the goods may be awarded. This is to account for any loss or depreciation during the period of wrongful possession.

(b) **Defendant No Longer Has the Goods.** When the defendant no longer has the goods, the primary remedy available is an award of damages. This compensation is typically calculated based on the fair market value of the goods at the time of conversion, providing monetary relief for the loss of the goods.

CHAPTER 2.
NEGLIGENCE

1. Definition and Fundamental Elements

Negligence is a situation where the defendant's failure to adhere to a required standard of care harms or damages the claimant.

To establish a claim of negligence, the following **key elements** must be demonstrated:

(a) **Existence of Duty of Care:** It must be shown that the defendant had a legal responsibility to exercise care towards the claimant.

(b) **Breach of the Duty:** The defendant did not meet their obligation to provide the standard of care owed.

(c) **Causation of Harm:** The defendant's failure to meet the duty of care directly caused harm or damage to the claimant.

2. Determining Duty of Care

The first critical step in a negligence claim is proving that the defendant owed a duty of care to the claimant.

2.1 Legally Recognised Duties

Through various judicial rulings, various scenarios and interpersonal dynamics have been legally acknowledged as situations where a duty of care exists. These duties are established and informed by precedent in case law.

An example of a legally recognised duty of care is a driver's responsibility towards other road users. This includes pedestrians, cyclists, and other drivers. The duty encompasses driving safely, adhering to traffic laws, and being alert to prevent accidents. For instance, if a driver runs a red light and collides with another vehicle legally crossing the intersection, this would breach their duty of care, potentially leading to a negligence claim.

2.2 Addressing New Duty Situations in Negligence

When encountering situations in negligence that lack precedent — termed new duty scenarios — courts are tasked with evolving the law cautiously, drawing parallels to established legal principles.

In determining the existence of a duty of care in these new contexts, **three pivotal elements** are considered:

(a) **Predictability of Harm.** The potential victim of the defendant's negligence must have been predictable, indicating the defendant's actions could foreseeably harm the specific claimant.

(b) **Closeness of Relationship**. A sufficiently close relationship, or 'closeness', must exist between the claimant and the defendant. Understanding the lack of such closeness can often be illuminated by cases where it is absent, such as in matters of purely financial loss or non-physical psychiatric harm.

(c) **Equitability and Justifiability.** Courts also weigh whether imposing a duty of care is equitable, justifiable, and reasonable within the context. This criterion allows the integration of broader policy considerations, ensuring the duty of care aligns with overarching legal and societal norms.

2.3 Duty Arising from Non-Action

In most cases, there is no legal obligation to take action. For instance, someone who witnesses another in peril is not legally required to assist them.

However, there are notable exceptions:

(a) **Duty from a Special Relationship.** A unique relationship between the involved parties can establish a duty to act. This is often seen in relationships like that of a parent and child, where there is an inherent duty of care. This duty can also emerge when the defendant voluntarily assumes responsibility for the claimant, creating an expectation of care.

An example of a special relationship creating a duty to act can be seen in the relationship between a school and its students. Schools have to ensure their students' safety while on school premises. If a student is injured on school grounds and the school fails to provide adequate care or assistance, this could be seen as a breach of the duty arising from their unique relationship.

Similarly, if a parent fails to provide medical attention to their child when required in a parent-child relationship, this could breach their legal duty to care for the child.

(b) **Duty Arising from Control.** A duty to provide care may be established when a defendant controls the claimant. A typical scenario is when a law enforcement officer detains an individual. In such cases, the officer assumes a duty of care towards the person under their control.

An example of a duty arising from control is when a police officer arrests a suspect. The officer assumes responsibility for the suspect's well-being while in custody. If the suspect is injured due to the officer's neglect (e.g., by failing to provide necessary medical attention after an injury during the arrest), this could constitute a breach of the duty of care owed by the officer.

(c) **Duty Linked to Control over Third Parties.** Usually, a defendant is not obligated to control a third party's actions to prevent harm to the claimant. However, this duty can emerge when the defendant has authority over the third party or has taken responsibility for their actions. For example, parents are generally expected to supervise their young children and could be liable if they fail to reasonably prevent their child from causing harm to others.

Consider a school that organises a field trip. Through its teachers and staff, the school has control and responsibility over the students during the trip. Suppose a student causes harm to another student due to a lack of adequate supervision. In that case, the school might be held liable as they have assumed responsibility for the student's actions during the trip.

(d) **Duty in Rescue Situations.** Although there's typically no legal requirement to perform a rescue, if a person chooses to engage in a rescue effort, they are obligated to avoid exacerbating the situation. Their duty is limited to not worsening the condition of the person or situation they are attempting to aid.

If a bystander sees someone drowning and decides to help, they have a duty not to make the situation worse. For instance, if the bystander attempts a rescue but pushes the person further underwater, this could be seen as a breach of their limited duty, as their action worsened the victim's situation.

3. Failure to Uphold Obligations

3.1 Evaluating the Standard of Care – The Reasonable Person Benchmark

After establishing that the defendant had a duty of care towards the claimant, the focus shifts to the level of care the defendant was expected to uphold. The required standard is reasonable care, akin to what a prudent person in the defendant's situation would have exercised.

This standard is objective and does not consider the defendant's attributes, such as their individual experience or lack thereof. Instead, the court assesses the nature of the defendant's activity and determines what actions a reasonable person engaged in the same activity would reasonably undertake or avoid.

3.2 Evaluating the Breach

To establish a breach of duty, an analysis is conducted post-incident. The claimant argues that harm resulted from the defendant's actions, which fell below the requisite standard of reasonable care.

The court's assessment of whether the defendant's actions were below a reasonable standard of care involves weighing **two primary factors**:

• **The Risk Level in the Defendant's Activity:** This considers the potential danger of the defendant's actions.

• **Feasibility of Taking Precautions:** This examines the practicality of implementing measures to mitigate the identified risk.

(a) **Evaluating Risk Magnitude.**

• **Firstly,** the court considers **Likelihood of harm**. If an activity poses a minimal risk of causing harm, and harm does occur, it might not constitute a breach of duty if the risk was so low that a reasonable person wouldn't have anticipated it. This assessment is based on the knowledge available at the time rather than hindsight.

• **Secondly,** the court considers **Severity of Potential Harm**. The more severe the potential harm, the greater the expectation for the defendant to take precautions. Even if the risk of occurrence is low, higher preventive measures are expected if the possible harm is significant.

(b) **Practicality of Taking Precautions.** The court considers whether it was practical for the defendant to mitigate the risk, balancing the ease and feasibility of such precautions against the risk.

(c) **Social Utility Consideration.** Reasonable precautions were reasonable, and the court also considered the social utility of the defendant's actions. For instance, in emergency or rescue scenarios, it might be suitable for the defendant to take fewer safety measures than would typically be required, given the urgent nature of the situation.

3.3 Assessing Breach of Duty for Specific Types of Defendants

The evaluation of breach of duty maintains an objective and impersonal approach. It's important to note that the expected standard of reasonable care is not adjusted based on the individual defendant's skills or experience.

Instead, the benchmark for proper care is set according to the nature of the activity or task the defendant engages in. This means that regardless of a defendant's capabilities or limitations, the legal standard applied is consistent with what is reasonably expected in the performance of that particular task or activity.

(a) **Responsibility of Under-Skilled Defendants.** Defendants who lack skills or experience cannot use this deficit as a defence for not meeting the required standard of care.

For instance, all drivers, regardless of their experience, are held to the standard of a competent, qualified driver. Even if the driver is a novice learner, their inexperience is not a valid excuse for failing to meet this standard. Suppose a learner driver does not drive at the level of an ordinary competent driver. In that case, they are considered to be in breach of duty despite their best efforts and limited abilities.

This principle extends to professionals undertaking tasks beyond their current skill level. For example, if a junior doctor takes on a more advanced role or task that demands a higher level of skill and competence, they are expected to meet the standards of that higher role. Their experience or skill level increases the standard of care required for their chosen task.

(b) **Expectations for Skilled Defendants and Professionals.** Individuals who practise a specific skill or profession, such as doctors or engineers, are held to the standard of a reasonably competent member within their respective fields. The benchmark for determining if such a defendant has breached the standard of care is based on whether their actions align with a responsible body of professional opinion. Initially established in the medical field, this approach applies to all professions requiring specialised skills.

- **Case of Failure to Inform Patients of Treatment Risks.** In medical treatment, consider a scenario where a doctor fails to inform a patient about the risks associated with a particular procedure. The treatment is performed competently, but the patient suffers harm from a risk that was not disclosed. In this situation, the doctor cannot justify failing to inform the patient by claiming adherence to a responsible body of professional opinion.

  The duty of a medical professional in this context is to responsibly inform the patient about material risks involved in a treatment, enabling the patient to make an informed decision. The criterion for what constitutes a 'material risk' is based on what a reasonable patient would deem significant rather than solely on medical opinion. This emphasises the patient's right to be aware of and consider potential risks in their treatment decisions.

(c) **Standard of Care for Child Defendants.** In tort law, there is no specified minimum age for liability. However, when the defendant is a child, their age significantly influences the expected standard of care.

This means that a child defendant is held to the standard of care reasonably expected of a typical child of the same age. This standard remains object-ive and does not consider the individual capabilities or maturity level of the specific child in question. Rather, the court assesses what level of care would be reasonably expected from an average child of that age. This approach acknowledges the variations in judgement, perception, and behaviour typical among children at different developmental stages.

3.4 Establishing Breach of Duty

The responsibility to demonstrate that the defendant breached their duty of care rests with the claimant.

(a) **Application of Res Ipsa Loquitur.** Typically, claimants present evidence, like witness testimony, to detail how the incident occurred, allowing the court to evaluate the defendant's level of care.

However, in situations where the incident details are unclear or unexplained, the court may infer a breach of duty based on the accident's circum-stances. This is where the principle of **res ipsa loquitur** (Latin for "the thing speaks for itself") comes into play.

For res ipsa loquitur to be applicable, **three criteria** must be met:

- **An unexplained cause** of the incident.

- The **object or situation** causing the accident was under the defendant's control.

- **The nature of the accident** is such that it would not ordinarily occur if due care had been exercised.

The invocation of res ipsa loquitur allows the court to presume negligence, aiding the claimant in establishing a breach of duty. However, this presumption can be countered if the defendant demonstrates that they exercised reasonable care.

(b) **Negligence in Criminal Convictions.** When an individual has been convicted of a criminal offence involving negligence, this conviction can be used as evidence in any related civil lawsuit. This provision streamlines establishing negligence in civil cases following a criminal conviction for the same incident.

4.Proving Damage in Negligence Cases

4.1 Establishing Harm as a Key Component

In a negligence case, demonstrating that damage or harm resulted from the defendant's negligent actions is crucial. The existence of carelessness alone on the defendant's part is insufficient for a claim; it must be coupled with actual loss or harm to the claimant. This means that the claimant needs to clearly show how the defendant's breach of duty directly led to their suffering or loss.

Establishing this direct connection between the defendant's negligent behaviour and the consequent damage falls squarely on the claimant. It is a central requirement in negligence claims, underscoring the necessity of actual harm or loss for the claim to be actionable.

4.2 Determining the Cause of the Claimant's Loss

For a negligence claim to be successful, the claimant must demonstrate that their loss resulted explicitly from the defendant's failure to uphold their duty of care rather than from an unrelated cause.

This involves a **three-part assessment:**

(a) **Factual Cause:** The claimant needs to establish that their loss would not have occurred 'but for' the defendant's breach of duty. This is the foundational step in linking the loss directly to the defendant's actions. In cases involving multiple causes for the claimant's injury, a modified approach to this test is applied.

(b) **Absence of New Intervening Acts:** It must be shown that no new, separate actions intervened between the defendant's breach and the claimant's loss. These intervening acts could break the causal chain established in the first stage.

(c) **Proximity of Damage:** The harm suffered by the claimant should be a reasonably foreseeable result of the defendant's breach. This step ensures that the loss is not too distant or unrelated to the defendant's actions.

These **two criteria** – the absence of new intervening acts and the proximity of damage – are collectively known as 'legal causation', distinguishing them from the factual cause established in the first step.

4.3 Establishing Factual Cause: The 'But For' Standard

The initial step in proving causation in a negligence claim is to establish, factually, that the claimant's loss directly resulted from the defendant's breach of duty.

This is determined using the 'but for' test. Essentially, the **question** is: **Would the loss have occurred without the defendant's breach of duty?**

(a) **Multiple Potential Causes.** The ' but for ' test remains applicable even in scenarios with several possible causes for the claimant's loss. The claimant must demonstrate that among these potential causes, the defendant's breach was the crucial factor leading to their loss.

(b) **Proof Requirement for Causation.** The claimant bears the responsibility of proving causation. The standard applied is that of the balance of probabilities, meaning the claimant must show that it is more probable than not that their loss was caused by the defendant's breach rather than by some other factor.

This requirement ensures that the defendant is held responsible only if it is more likely than not that their actions were the primary cause of the claimant's harm.

4.4 Adjusted Approach for Proving Factual Causation: Material Contribution

This approach differs from situations involving multiple alternative causes of the claimant's loss. Here, the focus shifts to cases where a single injury results from several concurrent causes. In such instances, the claimant is not bound by the 'but for' test.

Instead, the requirement is to demonstrate that the defendant's breach of duty significantly contributed to the claimant's loss. This 'material contribution' standard acknowledges scenarios where the defendant's actions and other factors collectively led to the claimant's harm. The claimant must show that the defendant's breach was a substantive factor in the resulting injury or loss, even if it was not the sole cause.

An example of the 'material contribution' test could be a medical negligence case where a patient suffers worsened health outcomes due to a combination of factors.

Imagine a patient, weakened by a pre-existing condition, undergoes a surgical procedure. During the operation, a surgeon makes a minor error; simultaneously, there is an unforeseeable complication. The patient's condition worsens significantly after the surgery.

Under the 'but for' test, it might be challenging to establish that the surgeon's error caused the patient's worsened condition, considering the pre-existing condition and the unforeseeable complication.

However, with the 'material contribution' test, the claimant (patient) must prove that the surgeon's error was a significant factor in the worsened outcome, even if it wasn't the sole cause. If the claimant can show that the error materially contributed to their deteriorating health alongside other factors, they can establish causation under this modified test.

4.5 Allocating Responsibility for Divisible and Indivisible Injuries

In cases where an injury is considered divisible, allocating damages among multiple defendants becomes possible based on the extent of the injury each defendant caused. This implies that the claimant may only obtain a fraction of their total damages from each defendant.

Therefore, to recover their losses fully, the claimant might need to pursue legal action against all responsible parties. This situation can have significant drawbacks for the claimant, especially if one or more defendants are financially insolvent or lack adequate insurance coverage.

For instance, if one of the defendants has gone out of business or doesn't have sufficient insurance, the claimant may be unable to recover the full extent of damages attributable to that particular defendant's actions, leading to a potential shortfall in the total compensation received.

An example of divisible injuries can be seen in occupational disease cases, such as hearing loss due to prolonged exposure to loud noise at different workplaces.

Imagine a worker, John, who has worked for three companies, each with varying noise exposure levels. After a medical diagnosis, it's determined that his hearing loss is partly due to working in these noisy environments. Each company contributed to some of his hearing damage, but not equally.

In this scenario, the injury (hearing loss) is divisible – it can be apportioned among the three companies based on how much each work environment contributed to the damage. If John seeks compensation, he must file claims against all three companies to recover the full extent of his damages.

However, suppose one of those companies has since ceased operations and lacks insurance. In that case, John might be unable to recover the total compensation for the portion of his hearing loss attributed to that company, ultimately receiving less than the total damages for his injury.

4.6 Sharing Liability Among Multiple Wrongdoers

In situations where an indivisible injury is caused by the actions of two or more defendants, and the claimant successfully obtains total compensation from one defendant, legal provisions allow for the apportionment of liability among all responsible parties. Specifically, the defendant who paid the total damages to the claimant has the statutory right to seek a financial contribution from the other co-defendants.

The court determines the amount of this contribution. It is based on what it considers fair and equitable, considering the degree of responsibility each defendant had in causing the damage. This mechanism ensures that the burden of compensation is distributed among all liable parties in proportion to their contribution to the harm rather than being shouldered entirely by one party.

An example of this would be a car accident involving multiple vehicles where the negligence of two drivers causes the claimant's injury.

Imagine a scenario where a claimant, Sarah, is injured in a multi-car accident caused by negligent driving from both Driver A and Driver B. Sarah sues both drivers but, for various reasons, only manages to secure total compensation from Driver A. In this case, the injury suffered by Sarah is indivisible – it's impossible to separate the harm caused by each driver.

Under the law, Driver A, who paid the entire compensation to Sarah, can seek a contribution from Driver B. The court will then determine what percentage of the total damages Driver B is responsible for based on their role in causing the accident. This could be a 50-50 split or any other ratio the court finds just and equitable, depending on the specifics of the accident, such as the degree of negligence exhibited by each driver.

Thus, while Sarah receives her total compensation from Driver A, Driver A can recoup a portion of this payment from Driver B, ensuring that the financial responsibility for the damages aligns more closely with each driver's contribution to the cause of the accident.

4.7 Responsibility in Cases of Sequential Injuries

This scenario addresses cases where a claimant initially suffers an injury and subsequently incurs a second, distinct injury that exacerbates the first. Unlike instances where multiple causes contribute collectively to a single injury, here we consider two separate injuries occurring successively, each with its cause.

In such cases, the defendant responsible for the second injury is only liable for how much their actions have aggravated or worsened the claimant's pre-existing condition. They are not held accountable for the entire scope of the claimant's condition but rather for the additional harm or deterioration caused by the second injury.

This principle ensures that the defendant in the second incident is only responsible for the specific damage attributable to their negligence rather than the cumulative effect of both incidents. The legal challenge lies in discerning the degree of exacerbation caused by the second injury, separate from the original condition.

An example of successive injuries can be illustrated in the context of medical treatment following an initial injury.

Imagine a scenario where a patient, Emma, breaks her leg in a car accident caused by Driver A's negligence. She undergoes surgery to repair the fracture, but the surgeon, Dr. B, performs the procedure negligently, leading to complications that worsen Emma's condition.

In this case, Emma initially suffered an injury (a broken leg) due to the car accident. The second, separate injury occurs due to the surgeon's negligence during the operation, which exacerbates her condition beyond the original injury from the car accident.

Driver A is liable for the initial injury (the broken leg). At the same time, Dr. B is responsible only for the additional harm caused by the surgical complications, not for the severity of Emma's current condition. This means that Dr. B's liability is limited to the extra damage or worsening of Emma's condition that specifically resulted from the surgical error. Emma, therefore, has separate claims against each defendant, corresponding to the extent of harm each caused.

4.8 Impact of New Intervening Acts on Causal Chain

In legal terms, when a subsequent act or event occurs between the defendant's initial act of negligence and the ultimate injury suffered by the claimant, this can disrupt the causal connection.

This disruption, known as "breaking the chain of causation," means that the defendant's original negligent act is no longer seen as the direct cause of the final injury or loss experienced by the claimant. As a result, the defendant may not be held liable for the additional consequences resulting from this new intervening act.

This principle acknowledges that certain events or actions can sufficiently alter the course of events so that the original negligent act cannot be deemed responsible for all subsequent outcomes. The intervening act must significantly change the outcome, making holding the original defendant accountable for the final state of affairs unfair or unreasonable.

An example of a new intervening act breaking the chain of causation can be seen in a medical treatment scenario following an accident.

Suppose a pedestrian, Alice is negligently hit by a car driven by Person A, resulting in Alice breaking her leg. She is taken to a hospital for treatment. However, while in the hospital, she contracts a severe, unrelated infection due to a hospital error, which leads to significant complications far beyond the original leg injury.

In this case, Person A's negligence is the direct cause of Alice's broken leg. However, the hospital's error in allowing Alice to contract a severe infection is a new intervening act. This intervening act (the hospital's error) breaks the chain of causation between Person A's initial negligence and the subsequent severe complications Alice experiences. As a result, while Person A would be liable for the initial injury (the broken leg), they would not be responsible for the additional harm caused by the hospital-acquired infection resulting from an independent, intervening act by the hospital.

(a) **Claimant's Actions as an Intervening Act**. If the claimant performs an action that intervenes in the chain of events, this could disrupt the causal link. For the claimant's actions to be considered breaking the chain of causation, these actions must be entirely unreasonable. It's crucial to distinguish this from the concept of contributory negligence, where the claimant's lack of reasonable care contributes to their injury, leading to a reduction in their damages.

However, suppose the claimant's actions after the initial injury are so unreasonable that they constitute a new, separate cause of the subsequent injury. In that case, they may not be able to recover any damages for that subsequent injury.

Imagine a scenario where a motorcyclist, John, is slightly injured due to a car driver's (Driver A) negligence. However, instead of seeking immediate medical attention, John, against all reasonable advice, decides to participate in a dangerous motorcycle race the next day. During the race, John crashes and sustains serious injuries, far more severe than those from the initial accident.

In this case, John's decision to partake in a high-risk activity after the accident, which was unreasonable given his condition, acts as a new intervening act. His actions are so imprudent that they break the chain of causation from the initial accident caused by Driver A. Therefore, Driver A might not be liable for the severe injuries John sustained in the motorcycle race.

(b)   **Intervention by a Natural Event.** Similarly, an intervening natural event can also break the chain of causation. If a natural occurrence independently contributes to or exacerbates the claimant's loss or injury, it may relieve the defendant of liability for the further damage caused by this event. In such cases, the natural event must be significant enough to be considered a separate cause of the additional harm.

Consider a situation where Contractor A negligently damages a property, leaving a wall partially unstable. Before repairs can be made, an unexpected, severe earthquake occurs, causing the wall to collapse entirely and damage other parts of the property.

Here, the earthquake is an intervening natural event. While Contractor A is liable for the initial damage to the wall, they are not responsible for the extensive damage caused by the earthquake. The earthquake acts as a separate, intervening cause that breaks the chain of causation, absolving Contractor A from liability for the additional damages.

4.9 Evaluating the Scope of Damage in Negligence

This stage in a negligence claim involves determining whether the damage is a distant consequence of the defendant's negligence. Even if the defendant's actions directly cause the claimant harm, the defendant is not responsible if the harm is too remote.

(a) **Reasonable Foreseeability Standard.** The critical test for remoteness is whether the damage was a reasonably foreseeable result of the defendant's negligence. If the harm was not a foreseeable outcome of the defendant's action, it is deemed too remote, and the defendant is not liable for it.

(b) **Foreseeability Exceptions.** There are notable **exceptions** to the foreseeability rule:

• **Egg Shell Skull Rule.** This rule applies if the claimant has a pre-existing condition that exacerbates the harm caused by the defendant's negligence. The defendant is liable for the entire extent of the harm, even if the severity was unforeseeable. This principle acknowledges that defendants must accept their victims as they find them.

Suppose a claimant with an unusually brittle bone condition suffers a fracture from a minor car accident. In that case, the driver responsible for the accident is liable for the severe injury, even though such a serious injury would not be foreseeable in a typical car accident.

• **Similar in Type Rule.** This rule covers cases where the type of harm is foreseeable, but the specific way it happens is not. The defendant remains liable as long as the general harm is predictable.

Imagine a situation where a contractor negligently leaves a hole uncovered, and it's foreseeable that someone might trip and fall. Suppose a pedestrian falls into the hole but sustains an unusually severe and rare injury due to a unique medical condition. In that case, the contractor is still liable, as the injury, while unique in severity, is similar in type to what was foreseeable.

These exceptions are crucial in ensuring that defendants are held accountable for the full range of harm their actions cause, even when the specific details of that harm are unusual or unexpected.

4.10 Overview of Establishing Causation in Negligence Claims

For a negligence claim to be successful, the claimant must demonstrate that they have incurred damage or harm. Crucially, this damage must directly result from the defendant's failure to meet their duty of care. The responsibility to prove this relationship lies with the claimant.

To establish causation, the claimant needs to demonstrate the following:

(a) **Factual Causation:** The claimant must show that, as a real matter, their damage or harm was a direct result of the defendant's breach of duty.

(b) **Legal Causation**: The claimant must establish that no intervening acts or events severed the causal link between the defendant's breach and the claimant's harm. It must be proven that the harm suffered was a reasonably foreseeable outcome of the defendant's breach. This means that the type of harm should have been predictable to someone in the defendant's position at the time of the breach.

Together, these elements form the basis for proving causation in negligence claims. They ensure that the defendant is held accountable for the harm that is directly attributable to their actions and within the realm of what could reasonably have been anticipated.

5. Counteracting Factors in Negligence Claims

5.1 Shared Fault: Contributory Negligence

Contributory negligence serves as a partial defence in negligence cases but does not apply to intentional torts like trespassing the person.

(a) **Explanation of Contributory Negligence.** Contributory negligence involves the claimant's failure to exercise reasonable care for their safety. This lack of care contributes to the harm they suffer.

(b) **Relation to the Cause of the Accident.** The claimant's lack of care doesn't need to have caused the accident itself. The critical aspect is that their failure to take reasonable care contributed to the extent or severity of the damage they suffered.

(c) **Implications of Establishing Contributory Negligence.** Under the Law Reform (Contributory Negligence) Act 1945, a finding of contributory negligence does not nullify the claim. Instead, it leads to a reduction in the damages awarded. The court adjusts the compensation based on how much the claimant's lack of care contributed to their harm, proportioning it in a manner deemed just and equitable.

Thus, while the defence of contributory negligence does not dismiss the claim, it significantly affects the claimant's compensation.

5.2 Accepting Risk Voluntarily (Volenti Non-Fit Injuria)

This defence, often summarised as "to a willing person, no injury is done," can entirely negate a negligence claim if the defendant demonstrates that the claimant willingly accepted the risk of the defendant's negligence.

For this defence to be applicable, **two critical conditions** must be met:

(a) **Awareness of Risk:** The claimant must fully understand the specific risk involved. This awareness implies understanding the nature and extent of the potential danger.

(b) **Voluntary Acceptance:** The claimant must have voluntarily consented to undertake the risk. This consent implies a deliberate decision to face the risk without coercion or undue influence.

However, it is essential to note that this defence has statutory exceptions. One significant exception is that the defence of voluntary assumption of risk does not apply to passengers in road traffic accidents. This statutory provision ensures that passengers, who often have little control over the situation, are not barred from claiming negligence due to their mere presence in a vehicle.

5.3 Limiting Liability Through Exclusion Notices

A defendant may attempt to limit their liability by displaying a notice indicating their intent to exclude liability. This approach is commonly employed by property owners or occupiers seeking to protect themselves from liability claims from individuals entering their premises.

Key points to note about the exclusion of liability include:

(a) **Non-excludable Liability for Death or Personal Injury:** Any attempt to exclude liability for death or personal injury resulting from negligence is legally ineffective in business operations. This means businesses cannot avoid responsibility for negligence that leads to severe harm or death, regardless of any notice or disclaimer they may display.

(b) **Conditions for Excluding Other Types of Damage:** When it comes to other forms of damage caused by negligence, exclusion is only permissible if it meets specific criteria of reasonableness and fairness. This statutory control is designed to prevent businesses from unreasonably disclaiming responsibility for damages that arise from their negligence other than those causing death or personal injury.

These statutory limitations ensure a balance between the rights of businesses to limit certain liabilities and the protection of individuals from negligent practices that could result in serious harm.

5.4 Defence Based on Illegality

The defence of illegality serves as a complete bar to a claim in tort law. This principle dictates that a claimant cannot seek legal redress or damages for harm arising directly from their illegal activities. The law does not allow individuals to benefit from a situation they have created through their unlawful actions.

If a claimant is injured while participating in a criminal act, they are precluded from recovering damages for that injury through the tort system. This defence is rooted in the legal doctrine that prohibits individuals from profiting or benefiting from their wrongdoing.

For instance, if someone is injured while committing a burglary, they cannot successfully claim negligence against the homeowner for their injuries. The illegal context of their presence and actions on the property nullifies their right to claim compensation for any harm suffered during the act.

This principle upholds the integrity of the legal system by ensuring that it does not endorse or reward illegal behaviour.

CHAPTER 3.
EXAMINING NEGLI-
GENCE RELATED TO
SOLELY FINANCIAL
HARM

This section addresses negligence claims where the claimant has suffered purely economic losses, distinct from physical injury or property damage.

The fundamental components required to establish a negligence claim are consistent, even in cases of pure economic loss.

These include:

(a)   **Duty of Care:** The defendant must have owed a duty of care to the claimant.

(b)   **Breach of Duty:** The defendant must have breached this duty.

(c)   **Causation of Damage:** The breach must have caused the claimant's loss.

However, assessing duty of care in cases involving pure economic loss involves specific considerations. These principles acknowledge the unique nature of financial loss, which can be less direct and more diffuse than physical harm and, therefore, require a more nuanced approach to determine liability. The law in this area aims to strike a balance between allowing legitimate claims and preventing an unmanageable expansion of liability for purely financial losses.

1. Understanding Pure Economic Loss in Negligence

Pure economic loss in tort law refers to financial losses not directly linked to physical injury or property damage.

This category typically includes:

(a) **Damage to Property Not Owned by the Claimant:** Financial losses resulting from harm to property the claimant does not own.

(b) **Costs from Defective Products:** Expenses incurred due to defects in products that the claimant has acquired.

(c) **Non-Consequential Financial Loss:** Financial losses that do not directly result from physical harm to the claimant or their property.

Fundamental Principle – Non-Compensability of Pure Economic Loss:

In negligence, the prevailing principle is that pure economic loss is typically not compensable. There is generally no duty of care established to prevent such financial losses.

However, there is an important exception: when the economic loss results from negligent misstatements, compensation may be possible if there's a special relationship between the defendant and the claimant.

Differentiating from Consequential Economic Loss:

In contrast to pure economic loss, consequential financial loss falls under the standard negligence framework. This means that the usual negligence principles apply if the financial loss is a secondary result of physical injury or property damage.

In such cases, the duty of care covers financial losses directly resulting from the initial physical harm or property damage.

2. Financial Loss Arising from Negligent Actions

Loss Due to Damage to Others' Property:

When a claimant incurs a financial loss due to property damage, they do not own; this loss is typically not compensable in tort law.

Suppose a tenant, Alex, runs a business from a rented property. If a third party negligently damages the building, causing Alex to lose business income, Alex's loss is considered pure economic loss since Alex does not own the damaged property. As such, this loss is generally not recoverable in tort.

Cost Arising from Acquiring Defective Products:

When a claimant buys a defective product, the cost of the defect itself is seen as pure economic loss, which is typically not recoverable in tort law.

If Sarah purchases a computer that malfunctions due to a manufacturing defect, the loss she incurs to repair or replace the laptop is pure economic loss. While she may have a claim under contract law against the seller or manufacturer, she cannot typically claim this loss under tort law.

In cases where the defective product is acquired through a contract (like a sale agreement), the claimant might seek damages for breach of contract, which could cover the cost of the defective product.

However, the claimant may not have a contractual remedy if the product was received as a gift or the contractual party is no longer available as a defendant (e.g., the company has ceased operations).

For instance, if a friend gifts Bob a new gardening tool that turns out to be defective, Bob cannot claim the loss under tort law since it's considered a pure economic loss. His recourse might be limited without contractual relationship with the manufacturer or seller.

3. Handling Pure Economic Loss from Negligent Mis- statements

This section deals with financial losses that arise not from physical harm or property damage but from incorrect or misleading statements.

When advice forms part of a contractual service, and the service provider breaches the contract (e.g., by failing to provide advice with due care), the claimant can claim these financial losses as damages for breach of contract.

If a financial advisor provides incorrect investment advice under a contract, and the client suffers financial loss due to this advice, the client can claim damages for breach of contract.

General Lack of Recourse in Tort:

Generally, if advice is given outside of a contractual context, such as free advice, a claim for pure economic loss in negligence is usually not viable.

(a) **Special Relationship as an Exception.** However, an exception exists in cases of a special relationship, characterised by:

- The advisor understands the specific purpose of the advice.

- The knowledge that the claimant will rely on the advice for that purpose without further verification.

- Actual reliance on the advice of the claimant.

- Reasonableness of the claimant's reliance on the advice.

In essence, this exception applies when there's an assumed responsibility by the advisor and reasonable reliance by the claimant.

A local accountant casually advises a friend to invest in a particular stock, without a formal agreement. The friend incurs a significant loss based on this advice. In this case, recovering losses through a negligence claim is likely only if a particular relationship can be established.

(b) **Extension to Service Providers.** This exception also applies to professional services. Professionals like solicitors or financial advisors, who assume responsibility professionally, may owe a duty of care even outside a contractual relationship.

If a solicitor negligently drafts a will, resulting in financial loss to the beneficiaries, they could be liable for negligence due to the professional responsibility assumed in drafting the will, even if there's no direct contact with the beneficiaries.

4. Assessing Violation of Duty and Damage Linkage in Viable Economic Loss Cases

In scenarios where a claimant successfully demonstrates that the defendant owed them a duty of care under the rules applicable to pure economic loss, the following steps involve:

(a) **Proving a Breach of Duty:** The claimant must show that the defendant did not meet the expected standard of reasonable care. This involves demonstrating that the defendant's conduct or actions were below what would be considered acceptable under the given circumstances.

(b) **Establishing Causation:** It is also essential for the claimant to prove that the defendant's breach of duty directly led to their economic loss. This requires applying the standard principles for causation in negligence, including the 'but for' test and considering whether the damage was a reasonably foreseeable consequence of the defendant's actions.

(c) **Addressing Defences:** Any defences the defendant raises should be considered after establishing breach and causation. These might include contributory negligence, voluntary assumption of risk, or any other relevant legal defences that could mitigate or negate the defendant's liability.

In essence, even in cases of pure economic loss, the fundamental framework of negligence - duty, breach, causation, and defences - remains applicable, albeit with specific considerations for the nature of financial loss.

CHAPTER 4.
LEGAL ASPECTS OF
PSYCHIATRIC INJURY

1.Defining Pure Psychiatric Harm

Pure psychiatric harm is a type of injury that impacts the mental health of the claimant, occurring without any direct physical injury. This harm can arise from the distress of being placed in a difficult situation due to the defendant's actions or witnessing harm to others caused by the defendant.

The harm might manifest as a Diagnosed Psychiatric Condition Resulting directly from the traumatic event or shock, or a Physical Condition Induced by Shock (for example, a miscarriage triggered by extreme emotional distress).

For a claim of pure psychiatric harm to be successful in negligence, the **standard elements** must be established:

(a) **Duty of Care:** The defendant owes the claimant a demonstrable duty of care.

(b) **Breach of Duty:** The defendant must have breached this duty.

(c)   **Causation of Damage:** The breach of duty must have directly caused the psychiatric harm.

In these cases, the principles determining the duty of care are specific and depend on the classification of the victim, as the law recognises different criteria for different types of victims in cases of psychiatric harm.

Differentiating Consequential Psychiatric Harm:

Consequential psychiatric harm refers to mental health issues that arise as a secondary effect of a physical injury caused by the defendant's negligence. Unlike pure psychiatric harm, consequential psychiatric harm is linked to an initial bodily injury.

For instance, a person might experience severe anxiety or depression following a physically damaging car accident, or they might develop post-traumatic stress disorder (PTSD) after suffering burns in a fire. In cases like these, the psychiatric condition is a direct consequence of the physical injury and trauma.

The critical distinction is that such consequential psychiatric harm does not necessitate separate rules for legal recovery. Instead, the standard negligence principles apply.

This means that the duty of care established for the physical injury inherently covers any subsequent psychiatric harm that develops due to that injury. The claimant must still prove the usual elements of duty of care, breach, and causation, but these are evaluated in the context of the physical injury and its repercussions.

2. Classification of Victims in Pure Psychiatric Harm Case

In legal claims concerning pure psychiatric harm, the law differentiates between two categories of victims, each subject to distinct duty of care considerations:

(a) **Primary Victims:** These individuals are directly within the zone of danger caused by the defendant's negligent act or reasonably believe themselves to be in such peril. This category typically includes people physically involved in the incident or at immediate risk due to the defendant's actions. For instance, a driver in a car accident caused by another's negligence is a primary victim.

(b) **Secondary Victims:** This group comprises individuals who are not in the danger zone but are affected by witnessing the aftermath or consequences of the defendant's negligence. Secondary victims are usually bystanders or witnesses who, while not directly endangered by the incident, suffer psychiatric harm from observing its effects. An example would be a person who witnesses a severe accident caused by someone else and subsequently develops a psychiatric condition due to the traumatic experience.

The distinction between primary and secondary victims is significant as it influences the application of the duty of care rules. For primary victims, establishing a duty of care is more straightforward due to their direct involvement or proximity to the danger. In contrast, secondary victims face more stringent criteria to establish a duty of care, reflecting the law's approach to balancing the need for fairness to claimants and preventing an unmanageable liability expansion.

2.1 Establishing Duty of Care for Primary Victims

In cases of pure psychiatric harm, primary victims are those directly involved or in the vicinity of the danger caused by the defendant's negligence.

The duty of care owed to these primary victims hinges on the **following considerations:**

(a) **Foreseeability of Physical Injury:** For a primary victim, a duty of care concerning psychiatric harm is established if there is a foreseeable risk of physical injury to them due to the defendant's actions. This means that the duty of care is recognised based on the potential risk of physical harm, irrespective of whether bodily injury occurs.

(b) **No Requirement for Foreseeability of Psychiatric Harm:** Unlike secondary victims, for primary victims, the psychiatric harm itself doesn't need to be a foreseeable outcome of the defendant's negligence. The critical factor is the risk of physical injury. Therefore, if a primary victim suffers psychiatric harm as a result of being in a situation where bodily harm is a foreseeable risk, the duty of care extends to cover this psychiatric harm.

This approach acknowledges the direct exposure of primary victims to harm and recognises that psychiatric harm can be a natural, albeit unforeseen, consequence of being placed in a dangerous situation.

For example, if someone is involved in a car crash caused by another driver's negligence, they are considered a primary victim. Suppose they subsequently develop a psychiatric condition, such as PTSD, due to this incident. In that case, the negligent driver owes them a duty of care for this harm, even if the risk of psychiatric harm was not initially foreseeable.

2.2 Criteria for Duty of Care Towards Secondary Victims

In cases of pure psychiatric harm, secondary victims are those who are not directly in the zone of danger but are still affected by witnessing an incident caused by the defendant's negligence.

The duty of care owed to such secondary victims is subject to more **stringent requirements**:

(a) **Foreseeability of Psychiatric Illness:** It must be reasonably foreseeable that a person with ordinary resilience ("of normal fortitude") would suffer psychiatric illness under the circumstances created by the defendant's actions.

(b) **Close Relationship Requirement:** The secondary victim must share a close relationship of love and affection with the person directly endangered by the defendant's negligence. Common examples include relationships between parents and children or spouses.

(c) **Proximity to the Incident:** The secondary victim must have been present at the scene of the accident or its immediate aftermath. This presence must be close both in time and space.

(d) **Direct Witnessing of Events:** The secondary victim must have directly perceived the events with their senses, such as seeing or hearing the incident or its immediate consequences, without the aid of media or second-hand reports.

A duty of care to a secondary victim is established only if all these criteria are satisfied. For example, suppose a person witnesses a close family member being seriously injured in an accident and meets the above conditions. In that case, they may have a claim for psychiatric harm as a secondary victim.

However, someone who learns about an accident involving a loved one through a third party or after some time has elapsed would only sometimes meet these criteria.

3. Boundaries of Duty of Care in Pure Psychiatric Harm Cases

3.1 Requirement of a Medically Recognised Psychiatric Condition

In claims of pure psychiatric harm, whether for primary or secondary victims, a crucial limitation applies: psychiatric harm must be a condition that is medically recognised.

This requirement is in place to ensure that the psychiatric harm claimed is significant and identifiable by medical professionals.

(a) **Recognised Conditions:** Examples of such conditions include Post-Traumatic Stress Disorder (PTSD), clinically diagnosed depression, or anxiety disorders. These are conditions with established diagnostic criteria in the field of psychiatry.

(b) **Exclusion of Milder Psychological Distress:** Less severe forms of psychological distress, like transient feelings of anxiety, alarm, or upset, do not qualify. The law requires a threshold of severity, typically necessitating a formal medical diagnosis, to consider a claim for psychiatric harm.

(c) **Exception in Cases of Physical Injury:** It is important to note that this limitation does not apply when the claimant has suffered physical injuries along with psychiatric effects. In such scenarios, a claimant can recover damages for psychiatric effects like nightmares or anxiety as consequential to the physical injury. These effects are considered part of the overall harm suffered due to the bodily injury and are recoverable under the usual negligence principles.

Always remember that in cases involving physical injury, the threshold for psychiatric harm is not as stringent. In contrast, for pure psychiatric harm claims, the harm must meet the criteria of a medically recognised condition.

Distinction Based on the Nature of Shock:

In cases of pure psychiatric harm, the law differentiates between harm resulting from a sudden, traumatic event and harm developing over a prolonged period due to on-going stress or shock.

For a duty of care to be owed to secondary victims, psychiatric harm must typically result from a sudden and shocking event. Gradual psychological harm that develops over time, such as the distress experienced while watching a loved one suffer due to the defendant's negligence, does not usually meet this criterion. An example would be the gradual emotional impact on a person observing the prolonged hospitalisation of a family member injured in an accident. In such cases, the law does not generally recognise a duty of care for the resulting psychiatric harm.

Recent legal developments suggest that the 'sudden shock' requirement may not be as rigid for primary victims. Notable cases involve scenarios where a mother suffers psychiatric illness as a result of stress and trauma experienced during and after a negligently managed childbirth.

In these instances, the mother is considered a primary victim, as the unborn child is part of her, and she is directly involved in the harmful event. Although the harm in such cases is not the result of a single, sudden shock but occurs over a more extended period, the law recognises a duty of care for the mother's psychiatric harm.

For example, a mother may develop a psychiatric condition as a result of the stress and trauma experienced during a prolonged and complicated labour, exacerbated by medical negligence. Although the harm unfolds over hours rather than in an instant, the law still acknowledges the duty of care owed to her for this psychiatric harm.

These nuances in the application of the 'sudden shock' requirement reflect the law's evolving understanding of how psychiatric harm can manifest differently for primary and secondary victims.

4. Violation of Duty and Link to Damage in Cases of Mental Harm

After determining that a duty of care regarding psychiatric harm exists, the claimant's next **steps** involve:

(a) **Proving a Breach of Duty**: The claimant needs to demonstrate that the defendant's actions or inactions fell below the expected standard of reasonable care. This involves showing that the defendant did not act as a reasonably prudent individual would have in similar circumstances.

(b) **Establishing Causation:** The claimant must prove that the breach of duty directly led to their psychiatric harm. This requires applying standard principles for causation in negligence cases, including the 'but for' test and considering the foreseeability of the harm.

(c) **Considering Defences:** Finally, the claimant must address any defences the defendant might raise. These could include arguments like contributory negligence or voluntary assumption of risk, which could potentially mitigate or negate the defendant's liability.

In cases of pure psychiatric harm, these steps are crucial to link the defendant's negligence to the claimant's psychiatric condition and to establish the legal basis for compensation. The process mirrors that in other negligence cases, albeit focusing on the specific nature of psychiatric harm and its implications.

CHAPTER 5.
LIABILITY OF EMPLOYERS IN NEGLIGENCE CASES

1. Implementation of Standard Negligence Criteria

In cases where employees pursue negligence claims against their employers, the established **principles** of negligence law are applied:

(a) **Established Duty of Care:** The employer-employee relationship inherently involves a duty of care. Employers are legally obligated to ensure their workplace is safe and to protect their employees from harm actively.

(b) **Demonstrating Breach of Duty:** To build a successful case, the employee must provide evidence that the employer failed to maintain the required standard of care. This could involve negligence in workplace safety standards, employee training, equipment maintenance, or adherence to safety regulations.

(c) **Linking Breach to Injury:** The employee must prove that their injury or harm directly resulted from the employer's failure to uphold their duty of care. The harm should be a foreseeable result of the employer's actions or inactions, not an unrelated or distant consequence.

In addition to these elements, the employer's potential defences, like the employee's contributory negligence or the employee's acceptance of known risks, must also be factored into the evaluation of the claim.

The concept of employers' liability in negligence is pivotal in ensuring workplace safety and upholding the rights of employees, holding employers accountable for their role in preventing work-related injuries and fostering a safe working environment.

2. Understanding the Employer's Duty of Care

2.1 Extent and Nature of the Employer's Responsibility

Employers are obligated to maintain reasonable care for their employees' safety. This duty, while significant, is not a guarantee of safety but rather a commitment to proper care.

The employer's duty encompasses various aspects of the workplace environment:

(a) **Provision of Safe Equipment.** Employers must ensure that all machinery and equipment are safe to use. This also includes supplying necessary protective gear and tools when required.

(b) **Maintenance of a Safe Workplace.** It is the employer's responsibility to ensure that the physical workplace is safe. This covers aspects like providing the work environment is free from hazards that could cause injury.

(c) **Employment of Competent Co-workers.** Employers must exercise care in hiring competent staff and providing adequate training. For example, suppose an employee is injured because a co-worker is untrained or engages in unsafe behaviour. In that case, the employer may be liable for not ensuring staff competency or addressing known dangerous behaviours.

(d) **Implementation of a Safe Work System.** This duty involves creating and maintaining a working system that minimises risks. It includes supervising employees effectively, enforcing safety protocols, and conducting risk assessments regularly.

The employer's responsibility extends to managing risks of psychiatric harm due to workplace stress. If it's foreseeable that an employee might suffer harm due to work-related stress, the employer must take reasonable steps to mitigate this risk.

2.2 Non-Transferable Responsibility of the Employer

The duty of care an employer owes to their employees is intrinsic and cannot be transferred or outsourced, even when tasks are delegated. This principle underlines the non-delegable nature of an employer's responsibility for employee safety.

(a) **Inherent Responsibility Despite Delegation:** While employers often need to assign specific tasks to employees or independent contractors, this does not absolve them of their duty to ensure a safe work environment. Delegating a task does not equate to delegating the associated duty of care.

(b) **Obligation to Oversee Delegated Tasks:** Employers must not only exercise care in their direct actions but also ensure that the individuals to whom tasks are delegated adhere to the same standard of care. This means actively monitoring and verifying that all aspects of the work, even those carried out by others, meet safety standards.

(c) **Breach of Duty Through Others' Negligence:** If an individual to whom a task is delegated fails to exercise reasonable care, resulting in harm to an employee, it is considered a breach of the employer's duty. The employer remains liable for any safety lapses, regardless of whether they personally carried out the task or not.

This concept reinforces the idea that employers bear ultimate responsibility for the safety of their employees and must maintain oversight and control over all workplace operations, regardless of how tasks are distributed within the organisation.

An example of the non-delegable duty of care in employment could involve a construction company.

Suppose a construction company, XYZ Construction, hires an independent contractor to install electrical wiring in a new building. XYZ Construction's responsibility is to ensure that all work on the site, including tasks delegated to contractors, adheres to safety standards. Despite this, the contractor did the wiring work negligently, leading to unsafe conditions that resulted in an electric shock injury to one of XYZ Construction's employees.

In this scenario, even though the electrical wiring task was delegated to an independent contractor, XYZ Construction cannot absolve itself of responsibility for the employee's safety. The company's duty to ensure a safe working environment remains intact despite the delegation. Therefore, XYZ Construction could be found liable for the employee's injury because it failed to provide that the contractor executed the task reasonably.

This example illustrates how an employer's duty of care is non-delegable and emphasises the employer's obligation to oversee all aspects of workplace safety, regardless of whether employees or outside contractors perform tasks.

3. Evaluating Employer's Breach of Duty Based on the Reasonable Employer Standard

In assessing an employer's breach of duty, the law sets the benchmark at the level of care expected from a reasonable employer.

This involves **several key considerations:**

(a) **Reference to Common Practices:** While the standard practices of other employers in the same industry are considered to determine if the employer met the standard of reasonable care, they are not the sole determining factor. The employer's actions are evaluated against the broader backdrop of what is generally expected in the industry.

(b) **Consideration of Individual Employee Circumstances:** The employer's duty extends to each employee individually. This means that the specific circumstances of each employee – such as their role, skill level, health conditions, and other personal factors – influence what constitutes reasonable care in each case.

(c) **Awareness of Risks:** In cases involving industrial diseases or similar risks, the time when the risk became known in the industry is crucial. Employers are expected to act on risks before they become aware of them rather than retroactively.

(d) **Handling of Latent Equipment Defects:** Issues arise when an employee is harmed by equipment with latent defects which are not identifiable even with reasonable care. Historically, if an employer had exercised due diligence in acquiring equipment, they wouldn't be liable for injuries caused by unseen defects.

Employer's Liability (Defective Equipment) Act 1969 addresses the issue of latent defects. Under this legislation, if an employee is injured by defective equipment during work, and the defect is due to a third party's fault (manufacturer or supplier), the employer is deemed negligent. The employee must still demonstrate the equipment's defect and connection to a third party's fault. Once established, the employer is considered to have breached their duty of care.

These elements collectively ensure that employers are held to a high standard of responsibility, accounting for

both general industry standards and the unique characteristics of their workforce and work environment.

4. Establishing Causation of Damage in Employers' Liability Cases

When an employee claims damages due to an employer's negligence, the employee must establish that the employer's breach of duty directly caused the harm they suffered.

The standard principles of causation in negligence apply:

(a) **Factual Causation ('But For' Test):** The employee must demonstrate that their harm would not have occurred 'but for' the employer's breach of duty. This step requires showing a direct connection between the employer's actions (or lack thereof) and the harm incurred.

(b) **Absence of Intervening Acts:** The employee must prove that no significant intervening events severed the causal link between the employer's breach and the employee's injury. This ensures that the employer is held responsible only for the consequences of their negligence.

(c) **Reasonable Foreseeability of Harm:** The harm suffered by the employee should be a type that could have been foreseen due to the employer's negligence. This step assesses whether the harm is too remote or a direct outcome of the employer's failure to provide a safe working environment.

By applying these rules, the legal process ensures that employees can hold employers accountable for injuries or harm resulting from workplace negligence, provided there is a clear and direct link between the employer's actions and the employee's harm.

5. Available Defences in Cases of Employers' Liability

Defences similar to those in general negligence cases apply to employer liability claims. However, the workplace's unique dynamics can affect these defences' viability.

Defence of Voluntary Assumption of Risk:

This defence argues that the employee was aware of and willingly accepted the inherent risks associated with their job. For this defence to hold, it must be evident that the employee understood the risks and voluntarily chose to undertake them.

Establishing this defence in an employment context is often challenging. Employees typically work under certain conditions or expectations that may not allow for a proper 'free choice' in accepting risks. This is particularly relevant in environments where employees might feel pressured to take risks as part of their job duties.

Contributory Negligence as a Defence:

In line with general negligence principles, if it's shown that the employee's lack of reasonable care contributed to their injury, there can be a proportional reduction in the damages awarded. This defence acknowledges the shared responsibility between employer and employee for maintaining a safe working environment.

Examples where this defence might apply, include situations where an employee disregards established safety procedures or misuses equipment, thereby playing a role in the cause or severity of their injury.

CHAPTER 6.
INDIRECT RESPONSIB-
ILITY IN TORT

1.Employer's Indirect Liability for Employee Actions

The most common form of vicarious liability occurs in the employer-employee relationship. Employers can be held liable for torts committed by their employees, given certain conditions are met.

The **key factors** to consider are:

(a) **Confirmation of a Tort:** It must be established that a tort, a wrongful act leading to civil legal liability, has been committed.

(b) **Identification of the Perpetrator as an Employee:** The individual who committed the tort must be an employee of the employer being held vicariously liable. This distinction is crucial as it differentiates employees from independent contractors, for whom employers are generally not vicariously liable.

(c) **Relation to Employment:** The tortious act must have been committed during employment. This means the employee's actions were related to their job duties or occurred during their work hours, even if they were not authorised or were explicitly forbidden by the employer.

Scope of an Employer's Vicarious Liability:

(a) **Torts Against Third Parties:** This includes any wrongful acts committed by an employee that harm customers, clients, or any other individuals who are not business employees.

(b) **Torts Against Co-Workers:** Employers can also be held responsible for torts committed by employees against their fellow employees.

Vicarious liability in the context of employment is a crucial legal principle that emphasises the responsibility of employers to ensure their employees act within the bounds of the law while performing their job duties. It is intended to provide a remedy to victims who suffer harm from the actions of employees acting within the scope of their employment.

An example of establishing a tort in a vicarious liability case could involve a scenario in a retail store.

Imagine an employee of a retail store, John, physically assaults a customer, Alex, during a heated argument over a product return. Alex decides to take legal action, not only against John but also against the retail store, claiming vicarious liability.

The act committed by John is a battery, a recognised tort involving physical harm or offensive contact.

For Alex's claim to be valid, the elements of the battery must be established. This includes proving that John intentionally performed an act that resulted in harmful or offensive contact with Alex without Alex's consent.

It's also necessary to consider any defences John might have. For instance, if John argues that he acted in self-defence, this could negate the battery claim. However, if no such defence is applicable or valid, the tort of battery stands.

With the tort established, the claim against the retail store for vicarious liability would then focus on whether John's act of assault falls within the scope of his employment. If it's determined that John acted within the course of his employment duties when the incident occurred, the store could be held vicariously liable for his actions. This would be the case even if the store had policies against such behaviour, as the assault happened during John's work hours in the workplace.

1.2 Determining Employee Status for Vicarious Liability

In vicarious liability cases, establishing whether the tortfeasor (the person who committed the tort) is an employee is crucial, as employers are typically only vicariously liable for torts committed by employees during their employment.

(a) **Historical Criteria.** Previously, courts would assess whether the employer had the right to control how the work was done. A high degree of control would suggest an employer-employee relationship. This involved determining if the individual's work was an integral part of the business (indicating employee status) or merely an accessory (suggesting independent contractor status).

(b) **Modern Approach – Economic Reality Test.** The current approach encompasses a broader evaluation of the working relationship, focusing on the economic reality rather than just control or integration.

Key factors include:

(a) **Personal Service:** Is there an obligation for the individual to personally perform the work in exchange for a salary?

(b) **Control:** Does the employer have authority over how the individual's work is executed?

(c) **Equipment and Uniform:** Who provides the necessary tools and equipment? Is there a requirement to wear a specific uniform provided by the employer?

(d) **Financial Risks and Rewards:** Which party bears the financial risks and stands to gain from the work?

(e) **Contractual Terms:** Are the terms of the contract consistent with an employer-employee relationship?

Determining the status of the tortfeasor as an employee or independent contractor is essential in establishing an employer's vicarious liability. The modern approach takes a holistic view of the working relationship, considering various aspects that reflect the true economic nature of the arrangement.

1.3 Assessing If an Employee's Tort Falls Within the Scope of Employment

Determining whether an employee's tortious act falls within their employment is crucial for establishing an employer's vicarious liability. The assessment concerns the connection between the employee's job responsibilities and their wrongful act.

Key considerations include:

(a) **Assessing Job Functions:** The court first identifies the range of activities or functions assigned to the employee by the employer.

(b) **Evaluating the Connection with Wrongful Conduct:** The court then examines if there's a substantial link between the employee's role and the tort committed to justify holding the employer vicariously liable.

Specific **scenarios** that are evaluated include:

(a) **Negligence During Work Duties.** Employees who act negligently while performing their work are typically still considered within their employment.

(b) **Criminal Acts by Employees.** The fact that an employee's tort is also a criminal act does not automatically negate vicarious liability. The focus remains on the relationship between the tort and the employee's duties.

(c) **Ignoring Instructions.** An employee's tortious act while contravening explicit instructions can still fall within the scope of employment, depending on how the instructions limit the employee's actions.

(d) **Journey Deviations.** An employee deviating from an authorised route can raise questions about the scope of their employment. Minor deviations usually don't change the employment context, whereas significant deviations might indicate the employee acted independently.

Consider a delivery driver employed by a company who takes a significantly longer route to make a personal stop. During this detour, they negligently caused a traffic accident. This situation could be viewed as the driver being on a 'frolic' of their own, acting outside the course of their employment.

The extent and purpose of the deviation are critical in determining whether the driver was still within the scope of their employment at the time of the accident.

2. Recognising Relationships Similar to Employment in Vicarious Liability

Recent legal developments have expanded the scope of vicarious liability beyond the traditional employer-employee relationship. This expansion acknowledges a third category: relationships that are not precisely employment but are sufficiently similar to warrant the imposition of vicarious liability.

Such relationships are described as 'akin' to employment, where the following factors are considered:

(a) **Activity Undertaken on Behalf of the Defendant:** The tort must have been committed during an activity that the tortfeasor (the person committing the tort) was carrying out on behalf of the defendant. This suggests the defendant had some level of involvement or benefit from the activity.

(b) **Integration into Defendant's Business Activities:** The activity performed by the tortfeasor should be an integral part of the defendant's business operations. This contrasts with activities that are part of the tortfeasor's independent business.

(c) **Risk Creation by the Defendant:** The assignment of the activity to the tortfeasor by the defendant should have created or enhanced the risk of the tort occurring. This factor examines the role of the defendant in facilitating the circumstances in which the tort was committed.

Additional **considerations** may include:

• **Defendant's Financial Capability:** The court might consider whether the defendant is better positioned than the tortfeasor to compensate the victim. This often relates to the defendant having more significant financial resources or insurance coverage.

• **Degree of Control:** How much control the defendant had over the tortfeasor's activities can be a significant factor. Greater control by the defendant can imply a closer relationship akin to employment.

This broader view of vicarious liability reflects an evolving understanding of modern working relationships and the need to ensure victims can seek redress from those in a position to prevent or minimise the risk of harm, even if they are not traditional employers.

2.1 Demonstrating a Close Connection in Akin-to-Employment Relationships

Establishing a relationship similar to employment is the initial step in proving vicarious liability. Additionally, this relationship and the tort committed must have a demonstrable close connection. The criteria for establishing this connection mirror those used in determining whether an employee acted within the scope of their employment.

Key aspects include:

(a) **Assessment of Job-Related Activities:** The court evaluates whether the wrongful act was committed. At the same time, the individual was engaged in activities related to their role or duties that are part of the relationship akin to employment.

(b) **Evaluating the Nexus between the Tort and the Relationship:** It must be established that the tortious act was not an isolated incident unrelated to the individual's functions or activities but was instead closely linked to their tasks or responsibilities.

(c) **Degree of Relevance to the Defendant's Objectives:** The connection is assessed based on how the tortfeasor's actions relate to the objectives or business activities of the defendant. The more aligned the wrongful act is with the intended outcomes of the defendant's enterprise, the stronger the argument for vicarious liability.

This two-step process of establishing a relationship akin to employment and then demonstrating a close connection with the tort ensures that vicarious liability is applied fairly and justly, particularly in complex working arrangements that don't fit the traditional employer-employee model. It clarifies the extent of liability in situations where the boundaries of professional responsibility and personal conduct might otherwise be blurred.

An example of establishing a close connection in a relationship akin to employment for vicarious liability could involve a scenario in a healthcare setting.

Suppose a healthcare organisation contracts with an independent healthcare provider, Dr. Smith, to deliver certain medical services at their facility. Dr Smith is not an employee but works under specific terms that integrate her services into the organisation's healthcare offerings. Dr. Smith negligently misdiagnoses a patient during her work, leading to harm.

Dr Smith is not an employee but works closely with the healthcare organisation, providing services that are integral to the organisation's offerings. This relationship could be seen as akin to employment.

The misdiagnosis occurred while Dr. Smith performed her healthcare facility duties, fulfilling her contractual obligations. This act is closely connected to her work for the organisation.

If a lawsuit is filed against the healthcare organisation for Dr Smith's negligence, the organisation might be held vicariously liable. The court would consider the nature of Dr Smith's relationship with the organisation and the circumstances of the misdiagnosis to determine if the organisation should bear responsibility for her actions, even though she is not a traditional employee.

This example illustrates how vicarious liability can extend to relationships resembling employment, especially when the wrongful act is deeply intertwined with the services provided.

3. Liability Concerning Independent Contractors

While employers are generally not vicariously liable for torts committed by independent contractors, there are circumstances where an employer may be personally responsible for a tort committed by an independent contractor. This liability arises from the employer's actions or inactions rather than a vicarious relationship.

Key scenarios include:

3.1 Situations Leading to Employer's Personal Liability

(a) **Breach of Non-Delegable Duty of Care:** Certain care duties are deemed non-delegable, meaning the employer cannot transfer the responsibility to an independent contractor. Suppose a tort occurs in an area where the employer has such a non delegable duty (e.g., ensuring safety in a workplace). In that case, the employer may be personally liable for breaches, regardless of whether they directly committed the tort.

(b) **Negligence in Selecting a Contractor:** Employers must exercise reasonable care when choosing an independent contractor. This involves ensuring that the contractor is competent and reliable. If an employer fails to vet a contractor properly, and this oversight leads to a tort, the employer may be personally liable for the resulting harm. This liability is based on the employer's negligence in the selection process, not the contractor's actions.

In both cases, the employer's liability stems from their failure to uphold a standard of care, whether in maintaining specific non-delegable responsibilities or in the prudent selection and oversight of independent contractors. This distinction from vicarious liability highlights the importance of employers carefully managing their responsibilities and decisions, especially when outsourcing work to separate parties.

3.2 Understanding Non-delegable Duties of Care

Delegable duties of care represent a significant aspect of liability, particularly when independent contractors are involved. These duties are such that an employer or principal cannot transfer the responsibility to another party.

Two key areas where non-delegable duties arise include:

(a) **Employer's Duty to Employees.** Even when employers hire independent contractors, their duty of care towards their employees remains intact. If an independent contractor fails to maintain reasonable care in a task that falls under the employer's non-delegable duty, the employer can be liable for any resulting harm. The liability here is not vicarious but stems from the employer's breach of their non-delegable duty to ensure safety and care for their employees.

(b) **Non-Delegable Duties in Other Contexts.** When an independent contractor is hired for particularly hazardous tasks (like highway construction or tasks inherently likely to cause nuisance), the entity employing the contractor has a non-delegable duty to ensure the activity is conducted safely.

Educational institutions have a recognised non-delegable duty of care towards their students. This means that schools are responsible for the safety and welfare of their pupils, even when activities are conducted by independent contractors or occur off school premises.

These examples of non-delegable duties highlight that specific responsibilities, particularly those involving safety and welfare, remain with the original duty-holder, irrespective of any outsourcing or delegation to third parties. This legal approach ensures that entities with the power to control or influence risky activities maintain ultimate responsibility for preventing harm.

3.3 Responsibility for Choosing a Competent Independent Contractor

When an entity, such as a business or organisation, hires an independent contractor, it is legally obligated to ensure that the contractor is competent in performing the required tasks safely and effectively.

Failure to fulfil this obligation can lead to liability:

(a) **Duty of Care in Contractor Selection:** This duty involves conducting due diligence to confirm that the independent contractor has the necessary skills, experience, qualifications, and resources to carry out the work safely and following legal and industry standards.

(b) **Liability for Negligent Selection:** If an independent contractor causes harm or commits a tort due to incompetence or lack of skill, and it can be shown that the entity failed to exercise reasonable care in selecting the contractor, the entity can be held liable. This liability arises not from the contractor's actions but from the entity's negligence in the selection process.

For example, if a company hires an independent contractor to handle hazardous materials without adequately verifying their credentials and experience in handling such materials, leading to an environmental spill or worker injury, the company could be liable for not ensuring the contractor's competence.

This underscores the importance of thorough vetting and assessment in the hiring process of independent contractors, especially for tasks that involve significant risks.

CHAPTER 7.
SOLUTIONS FOR IN-JURY AND FATALITY CLAIMS

1. Compensation for Living Claimants in Personal Injury Cases

1.1 Objective of Awarding Damages

In tort law, the primary goal of awarding damages for personal injury is to compensate the claimant, as much as possible through financial means, for the harm suffered due to the tort.

This compensation aims to restore the claimant to the position they would have been in if the injury had not occurred.

(a) **Pecuniary Losses:** These are tangible financial losses that the claimant has incurred as a direct result of their injuries. They include medical expenses, lost earnings, and other out-of-pocket expenses related to the injury. The law seeks to reimburse these losses fully.

(b) **Non-Pecuniary Losses:** These losses encompass intangible harms such as pain, suffering, and reduced quality of life, which cannot be precisely quantified in monetary terms. The legal system addresses these through monetary awards that serve as recognition and compensation for these significant but non-quantifiable aspects of harm.

1.2 Duty to Mitigate Damages

Claimants in personal injury cases are expected to take reasonable measures to reduce or 'mitigate' their losses.

This duty includes:

(a) **Seeking Medical Treatment:** Claimants are expected to obtain the necessary medical care to heal or stabilise their injuries, which can also prevent exacerbating the condition.

(b) **Seeking Alternative Employment:** If applicable, claimants should attempt to find suitable alternative employment if they cannot return to their previous jobs due to their injuries. This helps to minimise lost earnings.

The mitigation principle ensures that claimants do not receive compensation for losses that could have been reasonably avoided. This aspect of tort law underscores the injured party's responsibility to actively contribute to their recovery and minimise the financial impact of their injuries.

1.3 Compensation for Pecuniary Losses Due to Personal Injury

Pecuniary losses refer to the financial losses incurred by a claimant as a direct consequence of an injury caused by the defendant.

The claimant is entitled to recover damages for various types of financial losses:

(a) **Loss of Past Income.** This represents the income the claimant lost from the time of the injury up to the trial or settlement. Since this loss has already occurred, it can be calculated with precision. The calculation is based on the claimant's net loss of income, accounting for deductions like tax and national insurance. Any sick pay received, which offsets the loss of wages, is also factored into this calculation.

(b) **Loss of Future Income.** Future income loss accounts for the potential earnings the claimant will miss out on post-trial or settlement. This loss might be due to an inability to work at all or in the same capacity as before the accident.

• **Complete Inability to Work:** The court assesses the loss based on the claimant's annual pre-accident income (multiplicand) and the years they are expected to lose income (multiplier). Adjustments are made for receiving the sum in advance and life's uncertainties.

- **Limited Capacity to Work:** If the claimant can work but earns less, the difference between the pre-and post-accident salaries is used for the calculation.

- **Reduced Life Expectancy:** If the claimant's life expectancy is shortened due to the injury, compensation for the income they would have earned in the 'lost years' is considered. Deductions are made for personal living expenses they would have incurred in those years.

(c) Expenses:

- **Past Expenses:** These include medical costs, care expenses, necessary equipment, home adaptations, and extra travel expenses incurred from the injury to the trial or settlement, which can be precisely calculated.

- **Future Expenses:** The court assesses future expenses based on evidence, covering ongoing medical treatment, care costs, and other necessary expenses.

- **Cost of Care:** Both paid and gratuitous care provided by relatives are compensable. The care provider has no separate claim; the compensation forms part of the claimant's damages.

- **Medical Treatment:** The claimant can opt for private medical treatment over free NHS services without affecting the legitimacy of their claim for these expenses.

In all these cases, the overarching objective is to financially restore the claimant to the position they would have been in if the injury had not occurred, acknowledging that some aspects of loss, particularly non-pecuniary ones, cannot be fully compensated by monetary means.

1.4 Addressing Non-Pecuniary Losses in Personal Injury Cases

Pecuniary losses encompass the non-financial aspects of harm suffered due to injury, primarily focusing on the following:

(a) **Pain and Suffering**: This pertains to the physical and emotional distress caused by the injury. It includes the immediate pain experienced during injury and any ongoing discomfort or suffering during recovery.

(b) **Loss of Amenity:** Loss of amenity deals with the impact of the injury on the claimant's quality of life and ability to engage in activities. This might involve the inability to continue hobbies, sports, or other leisure pursuits that were part of the claimant's life before the accident.

Compensation for these losses is awarded to cover the past and the anticipated future impact on the claimant. The assessment process includes:

(a) **Court Assessment Based on Guidelines:** The court assesses these damages using established guidelines derived from past case precedents. These guidelines help quantify the monetary value of such intangible losses.

(b) **Consideration of Unconscious Periods:** If the claimant was unconscious and thus did not experience pain or suffering during a part of their ordeal, no damages are awarded for pain and suffering for that specific period.

However, the claimant is still entitled to compensation for the loss of amenity during that time, as this aspect of damage addresses the loss of the ability to engage in life's activities, regardless of consciousness.

This approach to non-pecuniary losses aims to provide a monetary acknowledgement of the intangible yet significant impacts of injury, recognising that while money cannot fully compensate for these aspects, it can offer a form of redress and acknowledgement of the suffering and loss experienced.

1.5 Compensation for Property Damage

In personal injury cases, compensation often extends to include damages for any property that belongs to the claimant and has been damaged or destroyed as a result of the tort:

(a) **Destruction of Property:** If the claimant's property is destroyed, the damages will typically reflect the cost of replacing the property. This calculation is based on the market value of a similar item at the time of loss.

(b) **Repair of Damaged Property:** If the property is damaged but not destroyed, the damages awarded will correspond to the decrease in the property's value, usually equating to the repair costs.

(c) **Consequential Costs:** The claimant may be entitled to recover costs associated with the damaged property, such as renting a replacement item. In contrast, their property is being repaired or replaced.

1.6 Understanding Damages Terminology

In the context of personal injury claims, damages are categorised into **two main types**:

(a) **Special Damages.** These damages can be quantified and calculated precisely during trial or settlement. They typically include tangible financial losses incurred by the claimant up to the trial date, such as past loss of earnings and expenses incurred due to the injury.

(b) **General Damages.** General damages are more subjective and are assessed by the court. They cover aspects that are not precisely quantifiable, such as future loss of earnings, future expenses, and non-financial losses like pain, suffering, and loss of amenities.

These classifications help in the detailed assessment of the full spectrum of losses and harms experienced by the claimant, ensuring a comprehensive approach to compensation.

2. Claims and Damages Arising from Death

In cases where death occurs as a result of a tortious act, **two distinct types** of claims can emerge, reflecting the legal implications of the victim's death:

(a) **Continuation of the Deceased's Claim for the Benefit of Their Estate.** If the claimant (the person who suffered harm due to a tort) passes away, the claim they initiated doesn't necessarily end. Instead, their cause of action can continue and be pursued by their estate. This means that the legal representatives of the deceased can continue the claim to recover damages that the dead would have been entitled to if they had lived. This includes compensation for the pain and suffering the deceased endured before death and any financial losses incurred due to the injury.

(b) **New Cause of Action for Dependents and Bereavement.** When an individual dies due to a tortious act, a new and separate cause of action arises, distinct from any claim the deceased might have had.

- **Dependents' Claim:** This new claim allows dependents of the deceased (such as spouses, children, or other dependents who relied on the dead for financial support) to seek compensation for their loss of financial support.

- **Bereavement Damages:** Besides the dependents' claim, a statutory provision allows for a fixed sum to be awarded for grief. This is typically available to a limited class of relatives, such as a spouse or parents (in the case of a minor).

These two types of claims reflect the law's recognition of the broader impact of a wrongful death beyond the individual victim, extending legal recourse to their estate and dependents. It aims to provide some measure of financial relief and recognition of loss to those affected by the death.

2.1 Perpetuation of Deceased's Legal Claims

When a claimant who has initiated a tort action passes away, their legal claim does not automatically terminate but continues for the benefit of their estate. This principle ensures that the rights and remedies available to the deceased are not extinguished upon death.

If a claimant suffers personal injury and subsequently dies (whether related to the injury) before their claim is resolved, their estate can continue the claim. The estate is entitled to pursue damages for the pain, suffering, and loss of amenity experienced by the deceased up until their death, as well as any financial losses like medical expenses and lost earnings incurred during that period.

The claim maintained by the estate cannot include damages for losses occurring after the claimant's death. Furthermore, there is no provision for a claim based solely on the event of death if the deceased died instantly without experiencing pain or suffering and without incurring property damage or loss of earnings.

Suppose the deceased had contributed to their injury through their negligence. In that case, this factor is considered in the same manner as it would be for a living claimant, potentially reducing the number of damages awarded.

(a) **Irrelevance of Cause of Death**. The continuation of the tort claim is independent of the cause of the deceased's death. The claim persists regardless of whether the death was a result of the injury from the tort or due to an unrelated cause.

(b) **Exception for Defamation Claims.** Defamation claims do not continue after the claimant's death, as these are considered personal to the injured party.

(c) **Survival of Actions Against Deceased Defendants.** Similarly, if a defendant in a tort action dies, claims against them can continue and be pursued against their estate. This ensures the defendant's death does not negate the claimant's right to legal redress.

2.2 Legal Provisions for Dependants and Bereavement Damages

When a claimant passes away due to a tort, the law allows for additional claims on behalf of the deceased's dependents and for grief.

These claims are distinct from the continuation of the dead's legal action:

(a) **Claims for Dependants.** This claim is designed to compensate the deceased's dependents (typically children or other family members reliant on the dead for financial support) for their loss. The claim is predicated on the notion that had the deceased survived; they would have continued to provide financial support to these dependents. The compensation aims to cover the financial shortfall resulting from the deceased's untimely death.

(b) **Bereavement Damages.** Bereavement damages are awarded to the deceased's spouse or parents (in the case of an unmarried minor child). The amount designated for bereavement damages is predetermined by statute and is intended to acknowledge the emotional loss suffered rather than to replace lost financial support.

(c) **Prerequisites for Claims.** These claims are contingent on the deceased having had a viable cause of action had they survived the injury. In other words, if the dead could have pursued a claim for their injury, their dependents can seek damages following the death.

Additionally, suppose the deceased was partially responsible for the incident leading to their death (contributory negligence). In that case, this will proportionately reduce the amount of damages awarded for dependants and bereavement, reflecting the deceased's part in the causation of the injury and subsequent death.

2.3 Reimbursement for Funeral Expenses

In cases where the wrongful act or negligence of a defendant results in the victim's death, the law provides for the recovery of funeral expenses.

The reimbursement of these expenses depends on who has borne the cost:

(a) **Expenses Paid by the Deceased's Estate.** If the funeral expenses are paid from the deceased's estate, they can be recovered under the Law Reform

(Miscellaneous Provisions) Act 1934. This act allows the estate to include the cost of funeral expenses as part of the claim that continues after the deceased's death.

(b) **Expenses Paid by the Dependents.** Alternatively, if the dependents of the deceased have paid for the funeral, they can claim these expenses under the Fatal Accidents Act 1976. This provision acknowledges the financial burden placed on dependents due to the untimely death and aims to alleviate some of that burden.

In both scenarios, the ability to recover funeral expenses is an essential aspect of the law's response to wrongful deaths, recognising both the emotional and financial impacts of such events on the deceased's family and estate. Including funeral expenses in compensation claims reflects a holistic approach to addressing the consequences of fatal accidents or incidents.

CHAPTER 8.
RESPONSIBILITY OF PREMISES CONTROLLERS

1. Overview of Occupiers' Liability

Occupiers' liability concerns the legal responsibilities of those who control or occupy land or buildings towards individuals who enter their premises.

In the UK, this area of law is primarily governed by **two key statutes:**

(a)   The Occupiers' Liability Act 1957 deals with occupiers' duties towards lawful visitors.

(b)   The Occupiers' Liability: This Act extends specific duties to non-lawful visitors, such as trespassers.

1.1 Scope of Liability: Condition of the Premises

Both statutes focus on the occupier's liability for harm caused by the physical condition of the premises rather than activities conducted on the premises.

Key points include:

(a) **Definition of 'Danger':** The Acts define liability as "danger due to the state of the premises or things done or omitted to be done on them". However, legal interpretation has narrowed this to focus on the state or condition of the premises themselves.

(b) **Exclusion of Activities:** The statutes should be more generally interpreted to apply to activities carried out on the premises. Therefore, if an individual is injured due to an activity rather than the condition of the premises, their claim would fall under general negligence principles rather than the occupiers' liability.

These Acts establish a framework for determining when and how an occupier is responsible for injuries or damage suffered by individuals on their property, emphasising the importance of maintaining safe premises for visitors and trespassers.

1.2 Classification of Individuals on Premises: Visitors and Non-Visitors

The duty of care owed by occupiers varies based on the legal status of the individuals on their premises.

This status determines which statute applies in the event of an injury:

(a)   **The Occupiers' Liability Act 1957 - Duty to Visitors.** This Act governs the duties owed to 'visitors', defined broadly as individuals the occupier has explicitly or implicitly invited or permitted to enter the premises. This includes guests, customers, and, in some cases, even individuals entering for specific statutory purposes who are considered visitors under the law.

(b)   **The Occupiers' Liability Act 1984 - Duty to Non-Visitors.** The 1984 Act addresses the occupier's responsibilities towards 'non-visitors'. This category primarily encompasses individuals who enter the premises without permission, commonly known as trespassers.

Typically, non-visitors are individuals not invited or permitted by the occupier to be on the premises. The most frequent example is trespassers. The 1984 Act explicitly outlines the level of care occupiers must extend to such individuals, acknowledging that even unauthorised entrants are owed a degree of protection against hazards on the premises.

The distinction between visitors and non-visitors underlines the legal recognition that occupiers owe a duty of care to all individuals on their premises, albeit to varying degrees based on the visitors' legal status. This differentiation ensures that occupiers maintain a basic safety standard on their property, reflecting that specific responsibilities come with controlling and using land or buildings.

2. Duties towards Lawful Visitors under the Occupiers' Liability Act 1957

The Occupiers' Liability Act 1957 outlines explicitly the obligations of occupiers towards individuals who enter their premises lawfully, known as visitors. This Act establishes a standard of care that occupiers must meet to ensure the safety of these visitors.

A visitor, in the context of the 1957 Act, is an individual who enters the premises with the explicit or implicit permission of the occupier. This permission can be direct (such as a personal invitation) or implied (such as the general public's access to a shop during business hours).

Examples of Lawful Visitors:

(a) **A guest is invited to a private home for a social gathering.**

(b) **A customer enters a store to browse or make a purchase.**

(c)   A ticket holder attending an event at a sports arena or concert hall.

The status of an individual as a visitor is contingent on them adhering to the terms under which they were permitted entry. Suppose a visitor exceeds these terms or engages in activities outside the scope of their permission. In that case, they may lose their status as a lawful visitor and be classified as a trespasser.

Understanding who qualifies as a visitor is crucial for determining the level of duty owed by an occupier. This duty involves ensuring that the premises are reasonably safe for the purpose for which the visitor is allowed to be there. The Act emphasises the need for occupiers to actively manage the safety of their premises actively, acknowledging the potential risks that visitors might face.

2.1 Identifying the 'Occupier' in Occupiers' Liability

Under the Occupiers' Liability Act, an 'occupier' is defined as controlling rather than owning the premises. Understanding who qualifies as an occupier is essential for determining who owes the duty of care to lawful visitors.

An occupier is typically the individual or entity controlling the premises. This control implies the ability to grant or deny permission for others to enter and use the space.

It's important to note that the occupier of a premise may not always be its owner. Control, rather than ownership, is the critical determinant. For instance, a tenant who leases a property has control and is thus considered the occupier. In contrast, the landlord, who might be the owner, relinquishes this status upon renting the property.

2.2 Scope of 'Premises':

The term 'premises' under the 1957 Act broadly covers land and any structures, including buildings, gardens, and even temporary or movable structures such as scaffolding or ladders.

2.3 Responsibilities Towards Lawful Visitors:

(a) **Unified Duty of Care.** The 1957 Act establishes a unified 'common duty of care' applicable to all lawful visitors, superseding previous legal distinctions among different visitor types.

(b) **Character of the Duty.** This duty entails reasonable care to ensure the safety of visitors for the intended purpose of their visit. It encompasses protecting visitors from harm and safeguarding their property.

(c) **Reasonable Care Standard.** The standard of care aligns with general negligence principles, considering potential harm risks and the practicality of safety measures. It also accounts for the level of caution expected from the visitors themselves.

Key considerations include:

• **Children:** Additional safety measures are required due to children's lower caution levels.

• **Professional Visitors:** Visitors in a professional capacity are expected to be aware of occupational risks.

(d) **Meeting the Duty.** Various aspects determine whether the duty of care has been adequately met:

• **Warnings:** Simply warning visitors about potential dangers does not entirely exempt an occupier from liability. The warning must be adequate for visitors to navigate the risk safely.

• **Use of Independent Contractors:** An occupier can fulfil their duty by hiring competent contractors. However, the occupier must reasonably ensure the contractor's capability and the quality of work, particularly for complex tasks.

In summary, the Occupiers' Liability Act 1957 mandates a comprehensive and standardised duty of care for all lawful visitors. This duty is centred around the principle of reasonable care tailored to the nature of the visitors and their activities on the premises.

2.4 Establishing Causation in Occupiers' Liability Cases

When a lawful visitor sustains damage or injury on-premises and successfully demonstrates that the occupier breached their duty of care, the next crucial step is establishing causation. This involves proving that the occupier's breach directly led to the damage or injury.

The principles for establishing causation in occupiers' liability cases align with those in ordinary law negligence:

(a) **Causation in Fact:** The visitor must demonstrate that the injury or damage would not have occurred 'but for' the occupier's breach of duty. This involves showing a direct link between the breach (such as a hazardous condition on the premises) and the injury or damage suffered.

(b) **Proximate Cause:** The injury or damage must be a reasonably foreseeable consequence of the occupier's actions or lack thereof. This means that the type of harm should be predictable, given the nature of the breach.

(c) **No Intervening Causes:** The visitor must show that no intervening events or actions broke the causal chain between the occupier's breach and the resulting harm. If an intervening cause is present, it could mitigate or eliminate the occupier's liability.

2.5 Potential Defences in Occupiers' Liability Cases

In cases concerning occupiers' liability, several defences may be available to an occupier accused of breaching their duty of care:

(a) Exclusion of Liability:

- **Statutory Controls:** While the 1957 Act allows occupiers to exclude liability, this is subject to statutory limitations, especially when the occupier is conducting business.

- **Non-Business Contexts:** Non-business occupiers have fewer restrictions and may have more freedom to exclude liability.

- **Adequate Notice:** To be enforceable, the exclusion must be explicit and specifically cover the damage. It must also be adequately communicated to the visitor as part of a contractual agreement or through visible, non-contractual notices.

(b) **Voluntary Assumption of Risk.** This defence applies when the visitor has voluntarily and knowingly assumed the risk associated with the hazard on the premises. The principles mirror those in ordinary law negligence, requiring that the visitor was aware of and accepted the specific risk.

(c) **Contributory Negligence.** This defence might apply if the visitor contributed to their harm through negligence. The principles are consistent with ordinary law negligence, potentially reducing the damages awarded to the visitor based on their share of responsibility for the harm.

3. Understanding Occupiers' Liability Towards Trespassers Under the 1984 Act

The Occupiers' Liability Act 1984 addresses the duty owed to non-lawful visitors, primarily trespassers. A trespasser is defined as an individual who enters or remains on premises without the occupier's permission or exceeds the limits of granted permission.

3.1 Occupier and Premises

The concepts of 'occupier' and 'premises' in the 1984 Act align with their definitions in the 1957 Act. The occupier is the person in control of the premises, and the premises include land and structures on it.

3.2 Conditions for Duty of Care

The 1984 Act specifies conditions under which an occupier owes a duty of care to trespassers. A duty arises only if:

(a) **Awareness of Danger:** The occupier knows or should reasonably know about the danger on the premises.

(b) **Awareness of Trespasser's Presence:** The occupier is aware, or should be, that trespassers may encounter the danger.

(c) **Reasonableness of Protection:** It is reasonable in all circumstances for the occupier to take steps to protect against the danger.

These provisions reflect a balanced approach to occupiers' liability, recognising that while trespassers do not have the same rights as lawful visitors, occupiers are responsible for preventing foreseeable harm, even those who enter their premises without permission. The duty to protect trespassers from harm is contingent on the occupier's awareness of the risk, the likelihood of trespassers encountering it, and the reasonableness of taking protective measures.

Imagine a large private estate with a beautifully landscaped garden and hidden well. The estate owner knows the well's existence, but it needs to be obscured by overgrown plants and easily visible. The garden backs onto a public park, and a broken section in the fence divides the estate from the park. Despite this, the owner must still repair the wall or place warning signs about the hidden well.

One day, a teenager, unaware of the private nature of the estate, wanders through the broken fence while exploring the park and accidentally falls into the concealed well, sustaining injuries.

In this scenario, under the Occupiers' Liability Act 1984:

Awareness of Danger: The estate owner knows the well and its risk, especially since it's hidden and not immediately noticeable.

Awareness of Trespasser's Presence: Given the broken fence and the proximity to the public park, it is reasonable to assume that the owner could anticipate the possibility of trespassers entering the property.

Reasonableness of Protection: Given the known risk of the hidden well and the likelihood of trespassers, especially with the broken fence, it would be reasonable for the estate owner to take protective measures. This could include repairing the wall, clearing the overgrowth to make the well visible, or placing warning signs to alert potential trespassers of the hazard.

In this case, the estate owner could be liable for the teenager's injuries because they failed to take reasonable steps to mitigate a known danger on their property, even though the teenager was trespassing.

3.3 Definition of Duty Owed to Trespassers Under the 1984 Act

When the conditions outlined in the Occupiers' Liability Act 1984 are met, indicating that a duty of care is owed to a trespasser, the nature of this duty is specific and tailored to the circumstances.

The critical **aspects** of this duty are as follows:

(a) **Scope of the Duty:** Care owed to a trespasser must take reasonable measures to ensure that the trespasser does not suffer injury due to the identified danger on the premises. This duty is focused solely on personal safety.

(b) **Reasonableness:** The standard applied is one of reasonableness, which varies depending on the particular circumstances of each case. Factors such as the nature of the danger, the feasibility of taking preventative measures, and the likelihood of trespassers encountering the danger are all considered in determining what constitutes 'reasonable care'.

(c) **Limitation to Personal Injury:** It's important to note that this duty extends only to preventing personal injury to the trespasser and does not include a duty to avoid damage to the trespasser's property. This limitation underscores the primary concern of the Act, which is the safety and well-being of individuals rather than property protection.

This defined duty reflects a balanced approach, recognising that while trespassers do not have the same rights as lawful visitors, occupiers are still responsible for preventing foreseeable and severe harm, even to those on the premises without permission. The Act thus imposes a fundamental level of care that occupiers must uphold to address known, significant risks on their property.

3.4 How an Occupier Can Fulfil Their Duty to Trespassers

Under the Occupiers' Liability Act 1984, the duty owed to trespassers is characterised by reasonable care.

This implies that the measures an occupier must take to discharge their duty depend on various **factors:**

- **Assessment of Risk:** The occupier must evaluate the level of risk that a particular danger on the premises poses to a trespasser. This involves considering both the likelihood of trespassers encountering the threat and the potential severity of harm.

- **Reasonable Precautions:** The actions required to fulfil the duty of care are appropriate under the circumstances. What is deemed suitable will vary depending on the specific situation, including the nature of the danger and the practicality of various preventive measures.

(a) **Use of Warnings and Deterrents.** One specific way an occupier can meet their duty of care, as highlighted in the 1984 Act, is through warnings or measures to deter trespassers from encountering the danger. This could involve clear signage indicating the presence of a hazard, such as a deep water body, unstable structures, or other potential dangers.

In addition to or instead of warnings, the occupier may implement physical measures to discourage trespassing or access to particularly hazardous areas. This might include fencing off dangerous areas or securing entry points to unsafe buildings.

3.5 Causation of Damage in Cases Involving Trespassers

Just like in general negligence cases, a trespasser who alleges that an occupier breached their duty of care must prove causation. This involves demonstrating that the injury or damage they suffered resulted from the occupier's failure to meet their duty.

The **principles** for establishing causation are:

(a) **Causation in Fact.** The trespasser must show that their injury would not have occurred 'but for' the occupier's breach of duty.

(b) **Proximate Cause.** The injury or damage must be a foreseeable outcome of the occupier's actions or inactions.

(c) **No Intervening Causes.** The chain of causation must not be broken by any intervening events unrelated to the occupier's breach.

Defences Available to Occupiers Against Trespassers:

(a) **Exclusion of Liability.** The Occupiers' Liability Act 1984 does not explicitly address whether an occupier can exclude liability for harm to trespassers. This lack of clarity means the ability of occupiers to exclude such liability remains legally uncertain.

(b) **Voluntary Assumption of Risk.** This defence applies if the trespasser voluntarily and knowingly assumed the risks associated with the hazard. It follows the same principles as in standard negligence law, requiring awareness and acceptance of the specific risk by the trespasser.

(c) **Contributory Negligence.** If the trespasser's actions contributed to their harm, the defence of contributory negligence might be applicable. Like other negligence scenarios, this defence would reduce the compensation payable to the trespasser proportionate to their contribution to the harm.

These defences provide a framework for occupiers to potentiate their liability in situations involving trespassers.

However, the uncertain legal standing regarding the exclusion of liability under the 1984 Act means that occupiers must carefully consider the extent to which they can rely on this defence.

4. Landlords' Duty of Care Under the Defective Premises Act 1972

The Defective Premises Act 1972 introduces specific responsibilities for landlords, distinct from the duties of occupiers under the Occupiers' Liability Acts.

This duty is particularly relevant when a landlord has transferred control of the premises to a tenant but retains specific responsibilities:

(a) **Scope of the Duty.** The duty applies to landlords when their tenancy agreement requires them to conduct repairs or grants them the right to enter the premises for maintenance purposes.

(b) **Applicability.** The duty concerns defects in the premises that fall within the landlord's repair obligations or rights. It applies when the landlord is aware, or should reasonably be, of such defects.

(c) **Owed to Whom?** The duty extends beyond the tenant to anyone reasonably expected to be affected by the defect. This includes visitors, family members, or even workers who enter the premises.

(d) **Nature of the Duty.** The landlord must take reasonable care to ensure that people are safe from personal injury or property damage resulting from known or reasonably discoverable defects. This standard of care aligns with general principles of negligence, requiring the landlord to address known risks in a timely and effective manner.

(e) **Risk Awareness.** A vital component of this duty is the landlord's awareness of the defect. If a landlord could not have reasonably known about a defect, they might not be held liable for injuries resulting from it.

The Defective Premises Act 1972 thus imposes a duty of care on landlords to maintain their properties in a safe condition, recognising that even when they do not occupy the premises, landlords can still significantly impact the safety of those who use their properties. This duty underscores the importance of regular maintenance and responsiveness to repair needs in property management.

CHAPTER 9.
TORTIOUS RESPONSIB-ILITY FOR FAULTY PRODUCTS

1. Interplay Between Tort and Contractual Claims for Defective Products

In cases where an individual suffers harm due to a defective product, they may have recourse through tort and contract law. Understanding the nuances and advantages of each legal avenue is crucial for effectively addressing such incidents.

Contractual Liability under the Sale of Goods Act 1979: This Act governs sales contracts and implicitly assures that goods sold are of satisfactory quality and fit for their intended purpose. Claims under this Act are based on these implied contractual terms.

1.1 Benefits of Pursuing a Contract Claim

(a) **Strict Liability Aspect.** One of the key advantages of a contract claim is the principle of strict liability. In this context, the claimant doesn't need to establish the seller's negligence; it suffices to demonstrate that the product was defective.

(b) **Scope of Recoverable Damages**. Contract claims uniquely allow for the recovery of damages directly related to the defective product. This aspect is particularly relevant since such damages, categorised as 'pure economic loss', are typically not recoverable in tort claims.

For those affected by defective products, pursuing a breach of contract claim can often provide a more direct path to compensation, mainly when the primary issue revolves around the product's inherent defects. This approach contrasts with tort claims, where the focus is on the negligence aspect and the broader implications of the defect, such as personal injury or damage to other property.

1.2 Understanding the Privity of Contract Restriction in Product Liability Claims

In product liability, the principle of privity of contract is a crucial factor in determining whether a claimant can pursue a breach of contract case. This legal concept significantly influences the claimant's options for redress for defective products.

(a) **Privity of Contract Explained.** Privity of contract necessitates a direct contractual relationship between the claimant (the injured party) and the defendant (the party responsible for the product). It's a cornerstone of contract law, ensuring that only parties involved in the contract can sue or be sued under it

(b) **Restrictions for Claimants.** Individuals who have not purchased the product directly generally lack a contractual relationship with the supplier. Therefore, they usually cannot file a breach of contract claim against the supplier for the defective product.

A purchaser's contractual relationship is typically with the retailer or immediate supplier, not the product's manufacturer. As a result, under standard contract law principles, a purchaser cannot directly file a breach of contract claim against the manufacturer due to the absence of a direct contractual relationship.

(c) **The Role of Tort Law in Product Liability.** Given these limitations imposed by the privity requirement, tort law becomes particularly significant in product liability. Tort law, especially negligence, can offer a pathway to compensation for injuries or damages caused by defective products, even without a direct contractual relationship between the claimant and the manufacturer or supplier. This aspect of tort law is vital for ensuring that individuals have recourse when they suffer harm from defective products, regardless of their direct contractual connections.

In summary, while the privity of contract limitation can restrict specific pathways in contract law for addressing product defects, tort law offers an alternative route, broadening the scope of potential legal remedies available to those affected by defective products.

Sarah purchased a new blender from a local electronics store. A few days later, while using it, the blender malfunctions due to a manufacturing defect, causing her hand to be seriously injured. Sarah wants to seek compensation for her injury.

Privity of Contract Issue: Sarah has a direct contractual relationship with the electronics store where she bought the blender, not with the manufacturer who produced it. This means she can claim against the store for breach of contract under the Sale of Goods Act, but not directly against the manufacturer, due to the lack of privity of contract.

Tort Law's Role: To seek compensation from the blender's manufacturer, Sarah can turn to tort law, specifically a negligence claim. She would need to prove that the manufacturer owed her a duty of care, breached that duty by manufacturing a defective product, and that this breach directly caused her injury. Tort law allows her to pursue a claim against the manufacturer despite the absence of a direct contractual relationship.

This example demonstrates how the principle of privity of contract can limit the scope of contractual claims in product liability cases, while tort law provides an alternative route for seeking redress, particularly against manufacturers.

2. Pursuing Product Liability Claims Under Common Law Negligence

When a defective product causes injury, claimants can pursue legal action under the tort of negligence.

This route requires proving several vital elements, each critical to establishing a valid negligence claim:

(a)   **Duty of Care.** The claimant must demonstrate that the defendant (typically the manufacturer or supplier) owed a duty of care to ensure the product was safe for its intended use. This duty extends to all parties reasonably foreseeable to use the product.

(b)   **Breach of Duty.** Next, it must be shown that the defendant breached this duty. In the context of product liability, a breach might occur during the design, manufacturing, or distribution phases, resulting in an unsafe product.

(c)   **Causation of Damage.** The claimant must prove that the defendant's breach of duty caused the injury or harm. This requires demonstrating a clear link between the product's defect and sustained injury.

In product liability cases under ordinary law negligence, the focus is on establishing that the injury resulted from a failure by the manufacturer or supplier to adhere to the required standard of care.

Unlike contractual claims, negligence claims in tort require proof of fault, making them more complex but potentially more broadly applicable, especially in situations where the privity of contract is absent.

2.1 Clarifying the Duty of Care in Product Liability Cases under Common Law Negligence

In cases of product liability under ordinary law negligence, the manufacturer's duty of care is paramount and is defined by **specific vital parameters:**

(a) **Consumer.** The manufacturer's duty of care is owed to the direct purchaser and anyone who could reasonably be expected to use or be affected by the product. This broad definition encompasses users, and those a defective product may indirectly impact.

(b) **Manufacturer.** The manufacturer, as the product's creator, bears the primary responsibility. This duty is based on the expectation that the product should be safe for use once released into the market.

Those who install or repair products also fall under this duty of care, as their actions can directly impact the safety and functionality of the product. Retailers are generally not under a duty of care in negligence for merely selling a product. However, if they are in a position where they should have inspected the product for visible defects, they may be obligated to do so, thereby assuming a duty of care.

(c)   **Personal Injury.** The duty of care aims to prevent personal injury resulting from product defects. This includes injuries directly caused by the product's malfunction or failure. Consequential economic losses related to the injury, like medical expenses, rehabilitation costs, or loss of income, are also covered under this duty.

(d)   **Damage to Property.** The duty extends to preventing damage to other property caused by the defective product. This highlights the manufacturer's responsibility to ensure that their product does not pose a risk to surrounding property. Notably, the duty does not cover damage to the defective product itself. Such damage is considered pure economic loss and falls outside the scope of recoverable damages under ordinary law negligence.

This framework establishes the responsibility of manufacturers (and others involved in the product supply chain) to ensure product safety. It outlines the potential legal consequences of failing to meet these obligations. It emphasises the legal protections available to consumers and others impacted by product defects.

2.2 Understanding Breach of Duty in Product Liability Negligence Cases

When pursuing a claim for a defective product under ordinary law negligence, establishing a breach of duty by the manufacturer is crucial. This involves demonstrating that the manufacturer failed to uphold the standard of care expected of a reasonable entity in their position.

To establish a breach of duty, the claimant must prove that the manufacturer did not adhere to the level of care expected of a reasonable manufacturer of similar goods. This encompasses both the manufacturing process and product design.

In cases where the defect is believed to have arisen during manufacturing, the claimant faces the challenge of accessing evidence, often controlled by the defendant. However, courts may infer negligence from the mere presence of a defect, reasoning that such defects typically result from a lapse in the manufacturing process.

Proving negligence in product design can be more complex. The claimant must show that the product's designers failed to meet the reasonable standard of care in their design decisions. Due to product design's technical and specialised nature, this can be particularly challenging for claimants.

The existence of a defect, especially one that leads to injury or damage, can sometimes be used to infer that there must have been a lapse in either the manufacturing or design process that constitutes a breach of duty.

These aspects underline the difficulties often faced by claimants in proving a breach of duty in product liability cases under tort law. Such challenges have led to the development of statutory regimes of strict liability, which ease the burden of proof on claimants by not requiring them to demonstrate the manufacturer's fault. This shift towards strict liability represents a significant evolution in the approach to product liability, aiming to provide better protection for consumers and users of products.

2.3 Causation of Damage in Product Liability Negligence Cases

In product liability cases under the tort of negligence, establishing causation is a critical component of the claim. The claimant must demonstrate that the damage or injury they suffered was caused by the breach of duty (i.e., the defect in the product).

The standard principles of causation in negligence apply. The claimant needs to prove that 'but for' the defective product, they would not have suffered the injury or damage. This involves showing a clear and direct link between the product's defect and the harm incurred.

2.4 Defences in Product Liability Negligence Claims

In cases of product liability under negligence, defendants may invoke standard defences applicable in negligence law:

If it can be shown that the claimant's actions contributed to the harm they suffered, the defence of contributory negligence may be used.

For instance, if the claimant continued to use a product despite being aware of its obvious defects, this might reduce or negate the manufacturer's liability. In such cases, the claimant's compensation could be reduced proportionally to their contribution to the harm.

Other standard defences in negligence, such as assumption of risk or voluntary assumption of risk, might also be applicable depending on the case's specifics.

These aspects highlight the importance of the causation link between the product's defect and the harm suffered and the potential for claimants' actions to impact the outcome of a product liability claim under ordinary law negligence. Understanding these principles is crucial for both claimants and defendants in navigating the legal landscape of product liability.

3. Strict Liability under the Consumer Protection Act 1987

The Consumer Protection Act 1987 (CPA) introduces a significant shift in product liability cases by establishing a strict liability framework. This means that the focus is not on the negligence or fault of the manufacturer but instead on the existence of a defect in the product itself.

Key Features of the CPA:

(a) **Strict Liability for Defective Products.** Under the CPA, if a product is found defective and causes damage, the manufacturer or supplier can be held liable regardless of whether they were negligent. This alleviates the burden on the claimant to prove that the manufacturer was at fault.

(b) **Definition of 'Defect'.** A product is considered defective under the CPA when it does not provide the safety which a person is entitled to expect. This includes considering how the product was marketed, any warnings or instructions provided, and its expected use.

(c) **Scope of Liability.** The strict liability under the CPA applies to damage caused by the defect, including personal injury, death, and damage to property (other than the defective product itself).

The CPA's strict liability regime represents a necessary protective measure for consumers, ensuring manufacturers and suppliers maintain high product safety standards. By shifting the focus from the manufacturer's conduct to the product's safety, the CPA simplifies the process for claimants seeking redress for harm caused by defective products.

3.1 Claimants under the Consumer Protection Act 1987

The scope of potential claimants under the Consumer Protection Act 1987 (CPA) is quite broad, encompassing anyone who incurs damage due to a defective product. This damage can include personal injury, death, or property damage (except for the defective product). The CPA's inclusive approach ensures that a wide range of affected individuals have recourse to seek compensation.

3.2 Defendants in CPA Claims

The CPA identifies specific parties who can be held liable for damages caused by defective products.

These include:

(a) **Producer:** The product manufacturer is generally considered the primary party responsible for ensuring the product's safety.

(b) **'Own Brander' or Marketer:** Any entity that brands or labels the product as their own, even if they did not manufacture it, is also liable. This often applies to companies that put their brand on products manufactured by others.

(c) **Importer:** Any person or company that imports the product into the country for business purposes is liable under the CPA. This is particularly significant for products manufactured outside the jurisdiction.

(d) **Joint and Several Liability:** If multiple parties (producers, own branders, importers) are responsible for the same damage, they are jointly and severally liable. This means that the claimant can pursue compensation for the total damages from any or all of them.

Under the CPA, suppliers are not typically direct defendants. However, they can be involved in the following **ways:**

(a) **Identification Request:** If a claimant cannot reasonably identify the producer, own broker, or importer, they can request this information from the supplier.

(b) **Timeframe and Practicability:** The request must be made within a reasonable period, and it must be impractical for the claimant to identify the relevant parties independently.

(c) **Supplier's Response:** If the supplier fails to provide this information within a reasonable period, they can become a potential defendant. However, if the supplier provides the requested information, the claimant can trace the supply chain to find the appropriate party to sue.

This framework under the CPA not only simplifies the process of seeking redress for claimants but also ensures that those involved in the production and distribution chain bear responsibility for the safety of their products.

3.3 Defining 'Defect' under the Consumer Protection Act 1987

The concept of a 'defect' in a product is central to liability under the Consumer Protection Act 1987 (CPA). A product is deemed defective when it fails to meet the safety standards that the public is entitled to expect.

To determine if a product is defective, **several factors** are considered:

(a) **Instructions and Warnings:** The presence, clarity, and adequacy of instructions and warnings accompanying the product are crucial. Adequate warnings about potential risks can influence whether a product is deemed safe.

(b) **Packaging and Marketing Purpose:** How a product is packaged and marketed helps define its intended use, informing safety expectations. The product's presentation and the information provided to consumers play a role in determining if a product is deemed defective.

(c) **Reasonable Expectations of Use:** Consideration is given to what actions with the product might reasonably be expected. This includes regular and foreseeable misuse of the product by consumers.

(d) **Timeline of Supply:** The state of scientific and technical knowledge when the product was supplied is relevant. A product might not be considered defective if the danger was unknown and could not have been detected given the scientific and technical knowledge when it was put into circulation.

Hot Coffee Scenario: A case in point is coffee served at a temperature hot enough to cause scalding. Despite the potential for injury, the coffee may not be considered defective if it aligns with the general expectation of consumers that coffee is served hot. The assessment would revolve around whether the temperature of the coffee was consistent with consumer expectations and industry standards at the time of supply.

The definition of 'defect' under the CPA focuses on the expected safety standards from the general public's viewpoint, considering various contextual factors. This approach balances between protecting consumers and acknowledging practical product use and safety expectations.

3.4 Understanding Damage Coverage under the Consumer Protection Act 1987

The Consumer Protection Act 1987 (CPA) specifies the damages that can be claimed when a defective product causes harm. However, it also sets clear boundaries on what constitutes recoverable damage, excluding certain types of damages from its coverage:

(a) Included Damages:

- **Death and Personal Injury:** The CPA covers damages resulting from death or personal injury caused by a defective product.

- **Damage to Other Property:** Damage caused by the defective product to property other than the product itself can be claimed, provided it meets specific criteria.

(b) Exclusions:

- **Damage to the Defective Product Itself:** Consistent with common law negligence principles, the CPA does not cover damage to the defective product. This type of damage is seen as pure economic loss and is typically recoverable only through contract law claims.

- **Business Property Damage:** CPAs focus on consumer protection. Therefore, it only covers property damage typically used for private purposes and primarily intended for the claimant's personal use. Damages to property used for business purposes are excluded.

- **Minor Property Damages:** The CPA sets a threshold for property damage claims, excluding those where the cost of the damage is below £275. This threshold is designed to exclude minor property damage claims from the scope of the Act.

(c) Implications:

• The CPA's focus on consumer safety and private property underscores its role in protecting individual consumers rather than businesses.

• By setting explicit exclusions, the Act aims to streamline the claims process and focus resources on more significant claims, reflecting its intent to address serious safety failures in consumer products.

Understanding these parameters is crucial for both potential claimants and manufacturers. It guides claimants on the types of damages they can seek under the CPA and helps manufacturers understand their liabilities regarding product safety.

3.5 Defences Available under the Consumer Protection Act 1987

In claims made under the Consumer Protection Act 1987 (CPA) for damages caused by defective products, several defences are available to defendants. These defences provide a means for manufacturers and suppliers to mitigate or avoid liability potentially:

(a) **Absence of Defect at Time of Supply.** The defendant can argue that the product was not defective when it was first circulated. This implies that the defect developed later, possibly due to factors outside the manufacturer's control.

(b) **Non-Business Supply.** A defence is available if the defendant can demonstrate that they did not supply the product during a business. This includes showing that they were not acting for profit and were not the product's producer, own brander, or importer.

(c) **State of the Art Defence.** Known as the 'development risks' defence, a defendant can claim that the defect was not detectable given the state of scientific and technical knowledge at the time of supply. This defence is narrowly interpreted, especially in cases where a product category is known to have potential defects that are undetectable at the time of supply.

(d) **Contributory Negligence.** As with general negligence claims, contributory negligence applies under the CPA. If it can be shown that the claimant's actions contributed to the harm they suffered, this may reduce the defendant's liability.

(e) **Inability to Limit or Exclude Liability.** Under the CPA, a defendant cannot limit or exclude liability for damages caused by a defective product. This provision ensures that claimants have an unimpeded path to seek compensation for harm caused by faulty products.

These defences provide a balanced approach, allowing for the protection of consumers while also giving manufacturers and suppliers avenues to defend against unjust claims. They play a crucial role in the legal framework governing product liability, ensuring that claims are evaluated fairly and in the context of each case's circumstances.

CHAPTER 10.
VIOLATION OF LEGAL OBLIGATIONS ENACTED BY STATUTE

1.Statutes Providing for Civil Liability

Specific statutes explicitly create the possibility for civil claims in the event of their breach. These statutes outline particular duties and, if breached, can result in civil liability.

Some notable examples include:

(a) **Occupiers' Liability Acts 1957 and 1984:** These Acts impose duties on occupiers of premises towards visitors and trespassers. Breach of these duties can lead to civil liability.

(b) **Consumer Protection Act 1987:** This Act creates a regime of strict liability for producers, own branders, and importers of defective products, allowing for civil claims in cases of injury or damage caused by such defects.

When a statute expressly provides for civil liability, the claimant's task is to demonstrate that the statute was breached and that this breach led to their harm. The process involves applying the specific provisions and requirements in the relevant statute.

This legal framework underscores the importance of statutory duties in various areas, from consumer protection to occupational safety. Breach of these duties has regulatory consequences and can lead to civil liability, providing a mechanism for those harmed to seek redress. Understanding these statutes and their responsibilities is essential for both potential claimants and entities subject to such statutory obligations.

2. Statutes Excluding Civil Claims for Breach of Duty

In contrast to statutes that expressly provide for civil claims, some legislation explicitly excludes the possibility of civil claims arising from their breach. This exclusion means individuals cannot directly base a civil claim on violating these statutes.

Exclusion under the Health and Safety at Work Act 1974:

A notable instance of such an exclusion is found in Section 47 of the Health and Safety at Work Act 1974 (HSWA), as amended by the Enterprise and Regulatory Reform Act 2013.

This provision plays a crucial role in shaping the landscape of workplace safety-related civil claims:

(a) **Exclusion of Civil Liability:** Section 47 explicitly states that breaches of duties imposed by the HSWA, as well as health and safety regulations derived from it, do not give rise to civil claims, except in cases where regulations explicitly state otherwise.

(b) **Impact on Employee Claims:** As a result of this exclusion, employees who suffer injuries cannot directly claim civil liability based on a breach of statutory duty under the HSWA. Instead, they must resort to traditional tort claims, specifically negligence, to prove their employer's fault.

(c) **Relevance of Health and Safety Regulations:** Despite excluding direct civil claims, health and safety regulations remain significant in negligence claims. The standards and duties outlined in these regulations inform what is considered reasonable care under negligence law. Compliance or non-compliance with these regulations can be a critical factor in determining whether an employer has met the standard of care required in a negligence claim.

This exclusion emphasises the need for injured parties to navigate alternative legal pathways, like negligence, to seek redress for workplace injuries. It underscores the distinction between regulatory compliance and the establishment of civil liability, highlighting the complexity of legal remedies available in cases of workplace injuries and safety breaches.

3. Civil Claims under Statutes Silent on Civil Liability

In cases where statutes impose duties but are silent on whether a breach leads to civil liability, courts thoroughly analyse the possibility of a civil claim.

This analysis involves several **vital questions:**

Parliament's Intent Regarding Civil Claims:

The court examines the statute's language and overall purpose to discern if Parliament intended to create a right to a civil claim. If the statute aims to protect a particular class of persons, this could indicate an intention to permit civil claims. The existence of other means of enforcement or remedies within the statute may influence the court's interpretation of Parliament's intent. Once the court determines that the statute may allow for civil claims, claimants must satisfy the following elements:

Claimant Within Protected Class:

Claimants must demonstrate that they fall within the class of persons the statute aims to protect.

Breach of the Statutory Duty:

Adherence to Statutory Standards: The court assesses whether the defendant breached the specific duty imposed by the statute, which may include strict liability in some cases.

Type of Damage Intended to Be Prevented:

Claimants must show that the statute was designed to prevent the type of harm they suffered. This requires aligning the claimant's damage with the statute's purpose.

In a situation where a statute mandates the transportation of waste in sealed containers to prevent environmental harm, and the defendant breaches this by using open containers, leading to damage (such as waste damaging a car's windscreen), the claimant must demonstrate that such damage aligns with the statute's protective intent.

Establishing Causation:

Finally, claimants must prove that their harm was directly caused by the defendant's breach of the statutory duty.

This framework offers a comprehensive approach to dealing with statutes silent on civil claims. It ensures that claimants who suffer harm due to breaches of statutory duties can seek redress, even without explicit legislative provisions for civil liability. The approach balances the need for statutory compliance with the availability of legal remedies for those affected by breaches.

CHAPTER 11.
DISTURBANCES OF RIGHTS: NUISANCE AND THE PRINCIPLE OF RYLANDS V FLETCHER

1. Public Nuisance Deals

Public nuisance concerns actions that affect the general public or a substantial section rather than individuals or small groups.

A public nuisance is an act that causes unreasonable interference with the general public's comfort, health, or safety. It's not just about personal inconvenience but concerns broader public rights and interests.

Examples:

(a) **Obstruction of Public Ways:** A typical example is the obstruction of a highway, hindering free and safe public passage.

(b) **Offensive Trades:** Activities that emit foul smells or loud noises affecting a large area, such as specific factories or industrial operations.

(c) **Environmental Disturbances:** Quarry blasting causing widespread dust, noise, and vibrations can be considered a public nuisance if it disrupts a significant area and population.

(d) **Isolated Incidents:** An isolated event can constitute a public nuisance if its impact is substantial and unreasonable. For example, a one-time event severely disrupting general comfort or safety could be classified as a public nuisance.

Who Can Sue for Public Nuisance?

(a) **Individual Claims.** Individuals can sue for public nuisance if they suffer specific and tangible harm beyond what the general public experiences. This harm must be distinct and not merely a shared inconvenience with the public.

(b) **Action by the Attorney General.** The attorney general can initiate legal action on behalf of the public. This generally aims to obtain an injunction to prevent the nuisance's recurrence. Such actions are taken in the interest of public welfare and safety.

Public nuisance as a tort is unique in that it straddles the line between individual and collective rights, recognising that specific actions can have a broader impact on the community beyond personal grievances. The ability to take legal action, either as an individual suffering clear harm or through public representation, underscores the significance of balancing individual rights with community well-being.

2. Characteristics and Types of Private Nuisance in Details

Private nuisance addresses the conflicts arising from one party's use of their land, which detrimentally affects another's enjoyment or use of their adjacent or nearby property.

Characteristics and Types of Nuisance:

Unlawful Interference refers to significant, persistent disturbances that unreasonably hinder the claimant's enjoyment or use of their property. These disturbances mustn't be one-off incidents but recurring or continuous.

Kinds of Damage:

(a) **Physical Damage:** This encompasses any physical harm to the land or structures, such as erosion, structural impairments, or water damage.

(b) **Amenity Disturbances:** Issues like persistent loud noises, pervasive odours, intrusive light, or dust accumulation fall under this category.

(c) **Property Encroachment:** Involves any physical intrusion onto the claimant's property, like overhanging structures or invasive tree roots.

(d) *Distinction from Trespass:* Private nuisance typically involves indirect interference without the necessity for intent, distinguishing it from trespass, which is direct and intentional.

2.1 Liability in Private Nuisance

Liability falls on the individual or entity whose actions or negligence led to the creation of the nuisance, regardless of their current connection to the land.

Occupiers of the nuisance-originating land are liable, which includes scenarios where employees or contractors cause the nuisance. Additionally, if a trespasser initiates a nuisance, but the occupier later adopts or fails to address it, they, too, can be held responsible.

2.2 Who Can Initiate a Nuisance Claim?

In private nuisance cases, the right to initiate legal action is linked explicitly to the claimant's legal interest in the property affected. This criterion is essential to determine who has the standing to sue for private nuisance.

Proprietary Interest Requirement: The claimant must have a legal or equitable interest in the land.

This requirement encompasses individuals who possess various forms of **property rights**, including:

(a) **Freehold Owners:** Individuals holding full property ownership have the unequivocal right to sue for any nuisance affecting their land.

(b) **Tenants:** Those with a leasehold interest, whether long-term or short-term, can bring forward a claim, as their right to use and enjoy the property is legally recognised.

(c) **Exclusive Possessors:** Even without formal ownership or a lease, a person in complete possession of the land (such as a lawful occupant with a right to exclude others) can sue for nuisance.

Exclusion of Non-Proprietary Occupants: Persons who occupy or use the land but lack a proprietary interest are generally barred from suing for private nuisance.

This **exclusion** applies to:

(a) **Family Members Without Property Rights:** Adult children living in their parents' house who don't have a legal interest in the property are ineligible to sue for nuisance affecting that property.

(b) **Lodgers and Employees**: Individuals like lodgers or employees who reside or work on the property but do not have any ownership or leasehold interest also fall outside the ambit of eligible claimants.

In summary, the ability to sue for private nuisance is closely tied to having a recognised legal stake in the land. This legal approach ensures that only those with a substantive interest in the property are entitled to legal recourse for disturbances affecting their use and enjoyment.

2.3 Assessing the Unreasonableness of Interference

In the context of private nuisance, the concept of "reasonableness" plays a central role in determining whether interference with using and enjoying land is unlawful. Courts must weigh the conflicting interests of property owners to establish what constitutes acceptable behaviour.

The **factors** influencing this assessment include:

(a) **Severity and Persistence.** This aspect assesses the strength and persistence of the nuisance. A higher intensity and prolonged duration typically tip the balance towards unreasonableness. For example, loud music played occasionally might be tolerable, but it becomes more likely to be deemed unreasonable if it's noisy and persistent.

(b) **Local Area Characteristics.** The neighbourhood's character is crucial in private nuisance cases, particularly when considering amenity damage like noise, dust, and odours. The courts assess whether the interference is unreasonable by taking into account the **typical conditions of the area**:

- **Amenity Damage:** In cases of noise, dust, and smells, the court evaluates the existing environment of the neighbourhood. For example, residents in a busy city street are generally expected to endure higher noise levels than those in a quiet rural setting. This reflects the principle that the prevailing conditions of one's surroundings should influence one's tolerance level for such disturbances.

- **Physical Damage or Encroachment:** The neighbourhood's character is not a determining factor when the nuisance involves physical damage to land or encroachment. In these cases, the focus is on the actual harm caused, regardless of the area's general conditions. For instance, if a factory's emissions damage a neighbour's garden, the fact that the garden is located in an industrial area does not excuse the nuisance. The emphasis is on the direct physical damage caused, irrespective of the neighbourhood's character.

This distinction underscores the legal system's attempt to balance the rights of individuals to enjoy their property with the practicalities of different living environments.

While some level of disturbance is expected in certain areas, direct physical harm is not tolerated, regardless of the location.

(c) **Sensitivity of the Claimant's Property.** The concept of abnormal sensitivity in the context of private nuisance addresses the issue of whether a claimant's particular susceptibility plays a role in determining if an interference is unreasonable.

In legal terms:

- **General Standard:** The courts evaluate nuisance claims based on what would be considered a reasonable level of interference for an average person. This approach ensures that the law doesn't cater to individuals with unusually high sensitivity or unique requirements that are not typical of the general population.

- **Abnormal Sensitivity Not Usually Considered:** If the claimant's use of their land is affected due to their own eccentric or unique sensitivities, and this sensitivity would not affect an average person in similar circumstances, the interference may not be judged as a nuisance. For instance, if a claimant is unusually sensitive to a certain level of noise that would be considered normal and acceptable to most people, this personal sensitivity does not typically render the noise a nuisance in legal terms.

- **Balancing Interests:** This principle helps balance a landowner's right to use their land for legitimate purposes and the neighbouring landowner's right to enjoy their property. The law protects individuals from significant and unreasonable inferences while ensuring that ordinary and customary land uses are not unduly restricted due to individual peculiarities.

(d) Malicious Intent. In the context of private nuisance, malice can significantly impact the legal assessment of whether a particular behaviour constitutes a nuisance. In this setting, Malice refers to a spiteful or ill-intentioned motive behind the defendant's actions.

Key points include:

- **Reasonable Use Transformed by Malice:** Even if a specific land use is ordinarily considered appropriate and lawful, it can become a nuisance if it is driven by malice. This is because the law considers the physical act, its impact, and its intent.

For instance, if a property owner plays loud music at a volume that would typically be acceptable but does so intending to harass or disturb their neighbour, this could transform an otherwise lawful act into a nuisance.

The critical factor is the deliberate intention to cause annoyance or harm.

- **Legal Implications:** When malice is established, it overrides other considerations that may deem the act reasonable. Courts are more likely to find an action constitutes a nuisance if it is shown that the primary purpose was to harm or irritate others rather than to enjoy or use one's property.

- **Proving Malice:** Demonstrating malice in a nuisance case can be challenging, as it requires evidence of the defendant's intent. This often involves showing that the defendant's actions had no purpose other than to cause distress or harm to the claimant.

(e) **Focus on Effect Rather Than Conduct.** In private nuisance cases, the focus is on the reasonableness of interfering with the claimant's use and enjoyment of their land rather than the defendant's conduct. This aspect differentiates nuisance from negligence.

Key points include:

- **Reasonableness of the Interference:** The core question in private nuisance is whether interfering with the claimant's property rights is reasonable. This is judged by the impact of the defendant's actions on the claimant's use and enjoyment of their land.

- **Defendant's Conduct Secondary:** Unlike negligence, where the defendant's level of care is crucial, in nuisance, a defendant can be liable even if they acted with reasonable care. What matters is the effect of their actions, not the care taken in those actions.

For instance, a manufacturing process might be conducted with all due care and in compliance with industry standards. However, if it emits odours or noise that substantially interferes with a neighbour's comfort, it could still constitute a nuisance.

- **Importance of Property Rights:** This approach emphasises the protection of property rights in nuisance law. Even well-intentioned and carefully conducted activities can be a nuisance if they significantly interfere with a neighbour's property.

- **Legal Implications:** This principle burdens land users to ensure their activities do not unreasonably interfere with others, regardless of the care or precautions taken. It reflects a balance between the right to use one's property and the obligation not to harm others' property rights.

2.4 Reasonable Foreseeability Principle in Private Nuisance.

In private nuisance cases, the concept of remoteness of damage plays a crucial role in determining the extent of a defendant's liability.

This principle is centred around the idea of reasonable foreseeability:

(a) **Reasonable Foreseeability:** The fundamental measure for remoteness in private nuisance is whether the type of damage incurred was reasonably foreseeable. This means that the defendant can only be held liable for damages that a reasonable person would have anticipated as a likely result of their actions.

(b) **Limitation on Liability:** If the damage caused is of a type that was not reasonably foreseeable, it is considered too remote. The defendant would not be liable for these unforeseen damages in such cases. This principle serves to limit the scope of a defendant's liability to consequences that could reasonably be predicted.

For instance, if a factory's emissions cause damage to nearby residences in the form of paint peeling or plant death, such damage could be reasonably foreseeable.

However, if the same emissions somehow caused an entirely unforeseen and unusual type of damage – say, interference with electronic equipment in the area – this might be considered too remote if it was not a reasonably foreseeable consequence of the emissions.

(c)   **Balancing Interests:** This rule balances the need to hold defendants accountable for the consequences of their actions with the recognition that it is unreasonable to hold them liable for highly unpredictable and unlikely outcomes.

2.5 Legal Responses and Limitations in Nuisance Cases

(a)   **Acquired Right Through Prescription.** Suppose the defendant has been continuously engaging in an activity that causes a nuisance for over 20 years without any legal challenge. In that case, they may have acquired a legal right to continue this activity. This defence hinges on the uninterrupted and continuous nature of the activity and the lack of previous legal action against it.

Suppose a factory has been emitting noise consistently for over 20 years, and no legal action has been taken against it by affected neighbours during this time. The factory could claim a prescriptive right to continue this activity as it has become an established part of the environment, assuming the noise level has been consistent and continuous.

(b) **Legislative Authorisation.** If a nuisance results from activities that a statute permits, courts must interpret the statute to determine if it is legally sanctioned and what remedies, if any, are applicable.

Imagine a scenario where a waste processing plant is set up following statutory guidelines and permissions. Suppose a nearby resident files a nuisance claim due to the smell emanating from the plant. In that case, the court will review the statutory permissions to determine if these permissions implicitly authorised the nuisance (the scent).

(c) **Irrelevance of Planning Permission.** Obtaining planning permission does not serve as a legal shield in nuisance cases. A nuisance action can still be valid even if the activity causing it has received planning approval from local authorities.

A property developer receives planning permission to build a commercial complex. Once operational, the complex causes significant traffic congestion, leading to a nuisance claim from neighbouring residents. The developer's planning permission does not provide immunity against this nuisance claim.

(d) **Ineffectiveness of the 'Coming to the Nuisance' Argument.** Purchasing property adjacent to an existing nuisance does not invalidate a subsequent nuisance claim. The pre-existence of a nuisance before the claimant arrived at the location does not constitute a valid defence against nuisance claims.

If a person buys a house next to a long-established poultry farm, which has always had a distinct smell, and then sues for nuisance due to the odour, the farm can't use the defence that the nuisance (the scent) was pre-existing. The new homeowner's decision to move next to the farm doesn't negate their right to file a nuisance claim.

2.6 Legal Remedies for Addressing Nuisance Issues

(a) **Court-Ordered Restrictions or Halts (Injunctions).** A claimant in a nuisance case frequently desires to compel the defendant to stop or modify the nuisance-causing activity. To achieve this, they may request an injunction. However, obtaining an injunction is not guaranteed. It is a remedy granted at the court's discretion, depending on whether it suits the situation.

(b) **Compensation through Damages in Nuisance Cases".** In nuisance cases, a court may award damages to the claimant as compensation for the harm suffered due to the nuisance. These damages are intended to offset the impact of the nuisance on the claimant financially.

(c) **Self-Help Remedy of Abatement in Nuisance Cases.** Abatement is a remedy where the claimant proactively addresses a nuisance. This action involves the claimant directly intervening to halt the nuisance, but they must restrict their actions to what is strictly necessary. If the reduction requires accessing the defendant's land, the claimant should provide notice and allow reasonable time for the defendant to rectify the issue. Failure to give notice could lead to liability for trespass.

Conversely, with appropriate notice, entering the land to stop the nuisance can be a valid defence against a trespass claim.

3. Strict Liability Under the Rule in Rylands V Fletcher

The rule in Rylands v Fletcher creates a strict liability scenario for escaping hazardous substances from a person's land during non-standard land usage. This rule differs significantly from the tort of nuisance as it does not necessitate a persistent condition.

Instead, even a single escape incident is enough to trigger liability under this rule. The defendant may be held accountable without proving negligence or intent in such cases.

3.1. Conditions for Rylands v Fletcher Liability

To establish liability under the Rylands v Fletcher rule, the following conditions must be met:

- Accumulation of a Hazardous Item: The defendant must have brought onto their land an item or substance that poses a risk of harm if it escapes. The potential for harm upon escape, rather than the inherent danger of the item, is critical.
- Non-Natural Use of Land: The defendant's land use must be non-natural. This broad concept en-

compasses activities or uses that are unusual or atypical in the context of the environment where they occur.

- Escape Causing Damage: The item or substance accumulated on the land must escape and subsequently cause damage. This escape doesn't need to be ongoing; even a single incident of escape that results in harm can trigger liability under this rule.

(a) **Hazardous Accumulation Requirement in Rylands v Fletcher.** For liability under the Rylands v Fletcher rule, the defendant must accumulate something on their property that could become hazardous upon escape. Crucially, the item itself doesn't need to be inherently dangerous. The potential for harm arises from its escape. A classic instance is the storage of a substantial quantity of water. While water is not inherently harmful, it can become a significant hazard if it escapes in large volumes. This principle applies to various substances or items that, under normal circumstances, might be harmless but pose a risk when they are not contained.

(b) **Non-Natural Use of Land in Rylands v Fletcher.** The rule in Rylands v Fletcher imposes liability when the defendant uses their land in a way that's considered non-natural or extraordinary. This means the defendant's activity must involve a particular usage that heightens the risk of harm to others.

An example of such non-natural use is the storage of substantial quantities of industrial chemicals. These are not typically found in a residential setting, and their storage inherently carries a greater risk of danger if they were to escape. The critical factor here is that the activity or use of the land deviates significantly from ordinary land use, thereby creating an increased potential for harm.

(c) **Escape and Damage in Rylands v Fletcher.** Under the rule in Rylands v Fletcher, for a defendant to be held liable, the item or substance accumulated on their land must escape and subsequently cause damage. This means the substance must move from where it was confined to a place outside the defendant's control. Furthermore, this escape must damage property or land; personal injury damages are not covered under this rule.

An example of such a scenario would be if water stored in a reservoir on the defendant's property breaks free of its confines and floods a neighbouring property, causing damage. The focus here is moving the potentially harmful material from a controlled to an uncontrolled environment and the damage it causes.

3.2 Absolute Responsibility Principle

Under this principle, the law imposes an automatic responsibility on the landowner for any harm caused by hazardous materials escaping from their property. This responsibility applies regardless of the landowner's intentions or carefulness. It is solely based on the fact that the dangerous item left the landowner's property and caused damage.

3.3 Limitation of Liability Based on Predictability

This aspect sets a boundary on the liability under the Absolute Responsibility Principle. It states that the landowner is only liable for damages that could have been logically foreseen due to the hazardous item's escape. If the damages are extraordinary or couldn't have been predicted, they are considered too distant from the cause, and therefore, the landowner is not held responsible.

This limitation ensures that the liability is reasonable and within the bounds of what could be expected from the nature of the hazardous material or activity.

3.4 Defences to the Rule in Rylands v Fletcher

(a) **Unexpected Interference by an Outsider.** A valid defence can be presented if the defendant can demonstrate that the escape resulted from an unpredictable act by an unrelated third party. For instance, if an uninvolved person maliciously manipulates a valve, causing a water tank to overflow on the defendant's property, this act can absolve the defendant of liability.

(b) **Natural Phenomenon Defence.** This defence applies when the escape is due to rare and unpredictable natural events that no reasonable precautions could have anticipated or prevented. An example might be an extraordinary, unforeseeable deluge leading to a dam breach.

(c) **Agreement to Risk.** If the plaintiff has knowingly and voluntarily accepted the presence of the hazardous substance, either explicitly or implicitly, they cannot later claim damages resulting from its escape.

(d) **Shared Fault.** If the plaintiff's negligence contributed to the harm suffered, this defence could reduce or eliminate the defendant's liability under the principle of contributory negligence.

(e) **Permission by Law.** Suppose a statute or legal authority explicitly allows the activity or the presence of the hazardous material that led to the escape. In that case, this can serve as a defence against liability claims. This aligns with similar defences available in cases of nuisance.

CHAPTER 12.
DEFAMATION CLAIM AND OTHER RELATED TORTS

1. Key Aspects of Defamation

(a) **Defamatory Statement.** A statement is defamatory if it harms the reputation of the individual or entity it refers to, exposing them to hatred, ridicule, or contempt or causing them to be shunned or avoided.

(b) **Reference to the Claimant.** The statement must be understood to refer to a specific individual or legal entity. This does not necessitate direct naming; it is sufficient if those who know the claimant can reasonably infer that the statement is about them.

(c) **Publication.** The defamatory statement must be communicated to someone other than the claimant. This includes any form of communication, such as spoken words, written texts, online posts, or broadcasts.

(d) **Defamation Claimants.** Both individuals and legal entities, such as corporations, can initiate defamation lawsuits. However, for entities, there are additional considerations regarding the impact of the defamatory statement on their business reputation or operations.

Once these elements are established, the focus shifts to potential defences, including truth, honest opinion, privilege, or publication on a matter of public interest.

2. Characteristics of a Defamatory Statement

(a) **Perception by Right-Thinking Society.** For a statement to be defamatory, it must be such that it would lower the claimant's esteem in the eyes of a reasonable, right-thinking member of society. This assessment involves considering how an average person, not overly critical or insensitive, would view the statement.

(b) **Requirement of Serious Harm.** According to the Defamation Act 2013, a statement is not considered defamatory unless it has caused or is likely to cause significant harm to the claimant's reputation. This addition to the law emphasises the necessity for the statement to have a substantial negative impact rather than trivial or minor implications.

(c) **Special Consideration for Commercial Enterprises.** For businesses and commercial entities, the harm from the defamatory statement must translate into or have a high likelihood of severe financial loss. This criterion reflects the recognition that reputation is closely tied to financial stability and performance for commercial entities.

In summary, a defamatory statement not only tarnishes the claimant's reputation in the eyes of the general public but also must inflict or potentially inflict significant harm, particularly measurable in terms of financial loss for commercial claimants.

3. Identification of the Claimant in a Defamatory Statement

(a) **Direct and Indirect References.** A statement is deemed to refer to the claimant if it explicitly or implicitly identifies them. This identification could be through explicit means like mentioning the claimant's full name or indirectly through a job title, nickname, initials, or other distinguishable references. The critical factor is whether the statement makes a reasonable person recognise the claimant.

(b) **Test of Reasonable Interpretation.** When there's uncertainty about whom the statement refers to, the resolution lies in determining whether a reasonable person, aware of the context, would understand the statement as referring to the claimant.

This assessment includes considering the knowledge and understanding of an average person in the community or the claimant's social or professional circle.

3.1 Accidental Reference and the Offer of Amends

(a) **Unintentional Defamation:** A defamatory statement can refer to the claimant unintentionally. For instance, the defendant might intend to speak about another individual with the same name or a fictional character, but it inadvertently points to the claimant. Such situations, while unintentional, do not automatically exempt the defendant from liability.

(b) **Statutory Mechanism for Rectification:** In cases of unintentional defamation, the law provides a pathway for rectification through an 'offer of amends.' This offer is a formal proposal by the defendant to correct the statement, apologise, and agree to compensation and costs, either mutually agreed upon or decided by the court.

(c) **Consequences of the Offer:** Acceptance of the offer of amends leads to the conclusion of legal proceedings, except for enforcing the agreed terms. If the offer is declined, it can serve as a defence for the defendant.

However, this defence fails if the claimant proves that the defendant was aware of the likelihood of the statement being misinterpreted as referring to the claimant and knew it was false and defamatory.

In essence, the section on referring to the claimant in defamation underscores the importance of clear identification in defamation cases. It provides a remedial path for unintentional defamation through the offer of amends.

4. Communication to a Third Party

(a) Essential Criterion for Publication. The essence of defamation lies in the spread of a statement that harms an individual's reputation. This requires that the statement is communicated to at least one person other than the claimant.

Direct communication between the defendant and the claimant, without any third-party involvement, does not fulfil the criterion of publication in a defamation context.

(b) Reputation Impact. The rationale behind the publication requirement is the protection of reputation, which inherently involves the perceptions of others in the community. Defamation law seeks to address harms inflicted on how an individual is viewed by others, not just in their own eyes.

4.1 Responsibility of Multiple Publishers

When multiple parties disseminate a defamatory statement, each one involved in its publication process can be held responsible. This includes individuals or entities contributing to making, editing, and distributing defamatory content.

In the context of media, the author of a defamatory article, the editor who approves it, and the publishing house that distributes it can all be considered publishers. Each party makes the statement available to the public, thereby sharing the liability for any defamation that ensues.

There is a recognised defence for certain publishers, particularly in cases where they may not have known or had reasons to see that they were involved in disseminating a defamatory statement. This defence, known as 'innocent dissemination,' is applicable under specific circumstances, primarily for intermediaries or secondary publishers like news vendors or internet service providers who may not have direct control over the content.

In summary, the publication element in defamation cases underscores the importance of the statement being made known to others, reflecting the law's focus on protecting an individual's reputation in the eyes of the community. The potential for multiple publishers to be held liable highlights the shared responsibility in preventing the spread of defamatory content.

4.2 Differentiating Libel from Slander

Libel and slander are two distinct categories of defamation. Libel refers to defamation in a permanent format, such as written text, while slander pertains to transient expressions, like spoken words or gestures. The permanence of libel typically makes it more severe and damaging to reputation.

(a) Understanding Damage in Defamation:

- **General Damage:** This represents the harm to the claimant's reputation itself. It assesses the overall negative impact on how the claimant is perceived in the community or society.

- **Special Damage:** This is a quantifiable financial loss directly resulting from the defamation. It involves specific economic harm that can be measured and attributed to the defamatory statement.

(b) Libel - Reputation Centric:

- **Actionable Per Se:** Libel claims inherently acknowledge the damage to the claimant's reputation without demonstrating specific financial loss. The Defamation Act 2013 imposes a seriousness threshold to ensure the alleged harm is substantial.

- **Including Special Damage:** While general damage is the primary concern in libel, claimants can also claim for any specific financial losses incurred.

(c) **Slander - Financial Loss Focus.** In slander cases, claimants must specifically show financial loss resulting from the defamation. This highlights slander's focus on the tangible, economic consequences of defamatory statements.

In instances where slander implies criminal behaviour punishable by imprisonment or suggests professional incompetence or unfitness, the requirement to prove special damage is waived.

5. Remedies in Defamation Cases

Compensatory Damages:

(a) **General Damages:** These are awarded for loss of reputation and aim to compensate the claimant for distress and harm to their reputation. General damages essentially affirm that the defamatory statement was unwarranted.

(b) **Special Damages:** These cover specific financial losses directly linked to the defamation, such as loss of business or employment opportunities.

Injunctions:

An injunction can be granted to prevent further publication or dissemination of the defamatory statement. This is a judicial order aimed at halting the continuation or repetition of defamation.

In defamation cases, remedies typically involve compensation for damage to the claimant's reputation (including any associated distress) and legal measures to prevent further harm by stopping the spread of the defamatory statement.

6. Potential Defences

In defamation cases, once a claimant successfully establishes the core elements for a defamation claim, the defendant has several potential defences available:

6.1 Truth

As per section 2 of the Defamation Act 2013, demonstrating that the defamatory statement is true is a complete defence. The responsibility to prove the statement's truthfulness lies with the defendant. The defendant's potential malice is irrelevant if the statement is proven true.

6.2 Honest Opinion

Section 3 of the Defamation Act 2013 allows for a defence if the statement is shown to be an opinion, not a fact, based on facts and if an honest person could have held that opinion.

6.3 Defence for Publication on Matter of Public Interest

Section 4 of the Defamation Act 2013 provides a defence for defamatory statements on matters of public interest, provided the defendant reasonably believed publishing the statement served the public interest.

6.4 Privilege in Defamation Cases

Privilege provides a critical defence in defamation cases, and it exists in two primary forms: absolute and qualified.

(a) **Absolute Privilege:** Absolute privilege is a complete defence against defamation claims, irrespective of the defendant's intent or malice. Occasions of absolute privilege include **Parliamentary Statements** where statements made by members of Parliament during legislative sessions are privileged, protecting the democratic process and free debate. Also it include **Judicial Proceedings,** where statements made during judicial proceedings, including remarks by judges, attorneys, witnesses, and parties to the case, are covered. This ensures openness and honesty in the judicial process without fear of defamation suits.

(b) **Qualified Privilege:** Qualified privilege applies under certain circumstances, provided the statement was made without malice. In this context, Malice implies an improper motive or lack of honest belief in the statement's truth.

These privilege defences are essential in defamation law as they safeguard critical communications from litigation in public and private spheres, thus encouraging open and honest discourse in parliamentary, legal, and specific professional settings.

6.5 Unintentionally Disseminated Defamatory Statements - Innocent Dissemination

The Defamation Act 1996, specifically section 1, provides a defence for those who have unintentionally disseminated defamatory statements, known as "innocent dissemination."

To successfully claim this defence, the defendant must demonstrate:

(a) **Non-authorship:** They were neither the author, editor nor the commercial publisher of the defamatory statement.

(b) **Reasonable Care:** The defendant exercised proper care concerning the publication.

(c) **Lack of Knowledge:** The defendant was unaware and had no reason to suspect that their actions contributed to the publication of a defamatory statement.

This defence aims to protect individuals who may inadvertently be involved in distributing defamatory material, such as booksellers, librarians, and newsagents, distinguishing them from commercial publishers who are typically not shielded by this defence.

6.6 Defence for Website Operators

Section 5 of the Defamation Act 2013 offers a specific defence for website operators regarding defamatory content posted on their platforms. The operator must prove they did not post the defamatory statement themselves to use this defence.

However, the defence is negated if the claimant can establish:

(a) **Identification Impossibility:** The individual who posted the statement cannot be identified.

(b) **Lack of Response to Complaint:** The website operator didn't respond appropriately to a complaint about the statement, as dictated by prescribed regulations.

7. Improper Disclosure of Private Information

The tort of misuse of private information provides redress when a claimant's personal information is disclosed improperly. This area of law seeks to reconcile the claimant's right to privacy with the defendant's right to freedom of expression, two fundamental but sometimes conflicting rights.

In these cases, the central question is whether the claimant had a legitimate expectation that the disclosed information would remain private. This expectation is assessed based on what a reasonable person with ordinary sensibilities would feel if the information were about them. Some types of information, like details about one's health, personal relationships, or finances, are generally recognised as inherently private.

However, even with a reasonable expectation of privacy, the defendant may still argue that the public interest justified the disclosure. This is a matter for the court to decide, and the law distinguishes between what the public may find interesting and what genuinely serves the public interest.

In resolving these cases, courts weigh the claimant's right to privacy against the defendant's freedom of expression. This balancing act is guided by Articles 8 (right to respect for private and family life) and 10 (right to freedom of expression) of the European Convention on Human Rights. Neither right is absolute, so the court must consider each case's circumstances carefully to determine the appropriate outcome.

7.1 Factors in Privacy Cases

In cases concerning the misuse of private information, **two critical aspects** are assessed to determine the viability of the claimant's case:

(a) **Reasonable Expectation of Privacy:** This consideration revolves around whether the claimant reasonably expects the information to remain private. The nature of the information is pivotal here. Certain information types, like health details, personal relationships, and financial matters, are inherently private.

For other information types, the criterion is whether a reasonable individual with ordinary sensibilities would expect privacy if the disclosed information pertained to them.

(b) **Balancing Freedom of Speech and Privacy:** The second factor involves assessing whether the defendant's right to freedom of speech should override the claimant's privacy expectations. This also includes evaluating whether the disclosure served the public interest. It's crucial to differentiate between what is of general interest and what merely interests the public. This distinction means that the public's curiosity or interest in information doesn't automatically justify its disclosure as being in the public interest.

The concept of public interest plays a crucial role in determining the outcome of a case involving the alleged misuse of private information. Even when a claimant has a reasonable expectation of privacy, the public interest factor can override this expectation.

Key points to consider include:

(a) **Court's Decision:** The court is responsible for deciding whether disclosing the information was in the public interest. This decision is not based on subjective notions but on legal principles and precedents.

(b) **Distinction Between Public Interest and Public Curiosity:** A significant aspect of this consideration is the distinction between what constitutes public interest and what simply piques public curiosity. Case law has established that something exciting or appealing to the public does not automatically make it a matter of public interest.

(c) **Criteria for Public Interest:** Determining public interest involves evaluating whether the disclosure of the information contributes meaningfully to a matter of public concern or debate. It goes beyond mere public fascination or the sensationalism of personal details.

7.2 Balancing Privacy and Freedom of Expression in Legal Context

In legal disputes involving the misuse of private information, courts are tasked with balancing two fundamental rights: the claimant's right to privacy and the defendant's right to freedom of expression.

This balance is guided by **two critical articles** from the European Convention on Human Rights, which are incorporated into English law via the Human Rights Act 1998:

(a) **Article 8 - Right to Respect for Private and Family Life:** This article protects an individual's right to privacy, ensuring everyone has the right to a private and family life, home, and correspondence. It safeguards personal data and dignity from unwarranted public scrutiny or exposure.

(b) **Article 10 - Right to Freedom of Expression:** This article upholds the freedom of expression, including the freedom to hold opinions and to receive and impart information and ideas without interference by public authority.

The **interplay between these two articles** requires a careful and contextual analysis:

(a) **No Absolute Right:** Neither the right to privacy nor freedom of expression is absolute. Each case presents unique circumstances requiring a nuanced approach to ensure a fair and just resolution.

(b) **Balancing Act:** The judicial process involves evaluating the extent to which each right is affected by the case's specific circumstances. The goal is to strike a balance where neither right is unduly compromised, respecting the essence of both privacy and freedom of expression.

(c) **Case-by-Case Basis:** Decisions are made on a case-by-case basis, considering factors such as the nature of the information, the means of obtaining and disseminating it, the motive behind the disclosure, and the impact on the individuals involved.

This balancing act reflects the complexity of modern legal challenges where individual privacy rights intersect with the principles of a free and open society. Courts must navigate these challenges delicately, ensuring that protecting one right does not unjustly infringe upon the other.

7.3 Legal Remedies for Misuse of Confidential Information

In cases where private information is misused, the law provides specific remedies to address the harm caused. These remedies serve to compensate the victim and prevent further breaches of privacy.

The **two primary legal remedies** are:

(a) **Damages:** This is financial compensation awarded to the victim for misusing their confidential information. Damages aim to compensate the claimant for any harm, including emotional distress, damage to reputation, or financial loss directly resulting from the breach of privacy. Damages are typically determined based on the extent of the harm and the nature of the information misused.

(b) **Injunction:** The court order prohibits further misuse or disclosure of confidential information. An injunction is a preventive measure aiming to stop ongoing or privacy breaches. Protect the claimant from additional harm that could result from the further dissemination of their private information. An injunction can be a crucial tool for safeguarding the claimant's rights in cases with an imminent risk of other publication or misuse of the information.

These remedies are designed to address the consequences of privacy breaches and to deter future violations, balancing the need to protect individual privacy rights against the interests of free expression and information dissemination.

CONCLUSION

As we have explored throughout "Tort" the intricacies of the legal framework are both profound and extensive.

In conclusion, let this book be both your guide and your invitation to engage deeply with the law. May it inspire you to continue learning, questioning, and shaping the legal landscape of England and Wales.

REFERENCES

Fafinski, S., Finch, E. (2023). Tort Law. Pearson.

Horsey, K., & Rackley, E. (2023). Tort Law. Oxford University Press.

Lunney, M. (2017). Tort law: Text and Materials. Oxford University Press.

ABOUT AUTHORS

Anastasia & Andrew Vialichka have authored a revered collection of study guides and quizzes (metexam.co.uk), addressing the full spectrum of topics tested by the Solicitors Qualifying Examination (SQE). Their portfolio encompasses thorough treatments of *Business Law and Practice, Dispute Resolution, Contract, Tort, Legal System of England and Wales, Constitutional and Administrative Law and EU Law, Legal Services, Property Law and Practice, Wills and the Administration of Estates, Solicitors Accounts, Land Law, Trusts, Criminal Law and Practice, as well as Equity.*

Authors' works are not only informational but also innovative, incorporating AI-based technology to enhance test preparation. This modern approach tailors learning to individual styles, aiding students to master both the theory and practice required for the SQE.

www.ingramcontent.com/pod-product-compliance
Lightning Source LLC
Chambersburg PA
CBHW061244220326
41599CB00028B/5534